Under La

The joys of life in rural Spain

by Andrew D Johnson

MAY + NORMAN

Published 2008
An earlier version of this story was published in electronic form in 2000 as "Olives and Almonds"

Published by **Figleaf, C/Corbetta 10, Suite 407, 03710 Calpe, Spain.**
E-mail info@figleaf.org

Cover design by Mark Johnson
www.dustyghost.com

www.figleaf.org

Under Latin Skies

About the Author

Andrew Johnson is principal of an international consultancy specializing in strategic thinking and executive mentoring. His background in the travel business provides a unique insight to the cultural blend that life in Europe is fast becoming.

He lives with his wife Kathy in a super villa overlooking the Spanish Mediterranean. They have two sons and two grandchildren, all still living in the UK.

Dedicated to Mark and Paul.
They didn't question our sanity!

Under Latin Skies

1 - He called me "Hombré"

My wife, Kathy, and I spent the first night in our converted Spanish farmhouse on the Tuesday. We'd put in a good selection of furniture and were just waiting for the builder to arrange the finishing touches. You know the sort of thing – a gas supply so that we could heat the water; a few doors so that when my mother in law came to visit us she would not have to whistle in the bathroom.

We were also keen to get rid of the mountains of debris that seem to accumulate around building sites. And this builder wasn't going to be allowed to bury it in the back garden the way some British builders have. But then even if he'd wanted to he wouldn't have found it so easy to do as this house was built on bedrock.

I had one of my usual "chats" with him the following morning – "How's the family?" "New car going well?" "The almond harvest is in full swing" etc. for several minutes. Then "Anyway I shouldn't be taking up your time. But just before I go I wonder if you could tell me where our doors are?" "And the gas supply?" He was amazed that these jobs were not completed! And as for the piles of debris … it seems that he had been let down – and he promised action.

By five o'clock we had successfully put up various fittings and hung a selection of pieces of art. No workmen had arrived to finish off those minor tasks, and we realized that we had gone all day without food. I suppose when you weigh as much as I do that should be no great hardship. But I find that over the years I've become rather accustomed to eating two or three times a day. Added to the hunger we knew that we had to get various bits of hardware to fit a few remaining items to the walls, and Kathy was really rather keen to visit that lovely lighting shop in Vera.

So, true to form, instead of popping up the road to the village shop to get some emergency rations we drove the 40 minutes down the valley to Vera, one of several larger towns, and close to the coast. We found the food and ironmongery that we were looking for quite easily, but it still took four hours to complete this little sortie.

That's how we came back to our hillside farmhouse at 9pm on that second evening to be greeted by the unexpected sight of lights blazing and doors flung wide.

In England we lived for many years in a smallish Hampshire village, where the neighbors do a super job of keeping an eye on each other's properties. But even in the UK we took to heart what our Neighborhood Watch team told us, and locked the house when we went out.

So here we were. Our house was obviously not in the state in which we had left it. In the UK this would mean one of two things – either our sons had thrown yet another unannounced party – or we had been burgled!

The truth is that at this very moment our sons probably were throwing one of those parties for which our Hampshire house had apparently become so famed. I say apparently, because the sort of party that achieved this infamy had our absence as an absolute pre-requisite! Mike, our vicar, used to wind me up by telling me how much he enjoys our parties, especially the ones that we don't attend. The neighbors, still concerned for our well being, welcome us home from our travels with stories of arrivals and departures in the small hours of the night and tell of the countless old cars, which populate our drive and every other hard surface around.

Mark and Paul –then aged 20 and 18 – really did try hard to comply with our pre-trip instructions. But somehow, every time, they used to drift into type almost as our car has reached the next village.

But now, driving up to our new Spanish home, we were not facing simple uncertainty. We were facing uncertainty ... in Spanish. Would my only "so so" Spanish cope with explaining a burglary of a half furnished farmhouse to the *Guardia Civil* – the Spanish military police? What is the Spanish for "burglar" anyway? And what would I do if they had nicked the dictionary?

We had been told what an honest and trustworthy society we had chosen for this new chapter of our lives. How most houses locally don't even have locks. And how the only local villainy had been undertaken years before around 15 miles away by a chap with rather a sad life, who was so short on self-confidence that he always tried to put back everything he had stolen before the property owners noticed that it had gone. He apparently died of a broken heart brought on by the lack of a life partner. And,

being a magpie, he had rather beautiful purple and white plumage.
All this went through my mind in the few seconds it takes to reach the top of the hill from the point where our house "*Cortijo la Higuera*" first comes into view. If I'd had just a few more moments' preparation I would have worked out that this was a good sign - a sign of hope. It could only mean that the house must be populated by workmen laboring away.
So we drove around the back of the house and sure enough there was Pedro, the painter. But hold on a minute we weren't expecting any decorating jobs to be completed this week! I was confused - and tired. And despite our convoluted 4 hour to and from Vera, we still had not eaten.
It seems that Pedro was the reason that we had no doors. He had taken them all to be varnished and then disappeared on vacation. He'd varnished them all perfectly, and then, for safety's sake, had locked them away in his garage. Indeed he had done such a good job that Kathy's father, David, himself no mean decorator, was genuinely impressed. And now here Pedro was at gone 9 o'clock at night just starting to re-hang these doors - plus the doors that the carpenter had made for the kitchen cupboards and various other built in storage spaces.
But Pedro was not alone. As we walked in through our new front door we were welcomed by our neighbor, Andréas. We had been so busy all day that we had forgotten to pop in to tell Andréas that we were moving in at last. Over the previous 8 months he had seen us come and go on numerous occasions and we always tried to make a point of passing a few minutes with him. Now here he was keeping an eye on our property and telling Pedro how we rely on him.
It was clear from the start that Andréas was just the sort of neighbor you need. Like our neighbor Bill in England he seemed able to turn his hands to a number of craft skills way beyond my grammar school woodwork. To be fair our woodwork teacher, Mr. Danvers ("Dan Dan the Woodwork Man"), taught us a number of things. They centered on keeping our workspace clean and clear (good health and safety training) and checking that the tool store at the end of each bench contained the correct inventory of tools at the end of each lesson. One of my abiding memories of school is Mr. Danvers reciting the checklist of tools for us to verify, and ending, always, with "and finally either a hammer or a brush".
But having established long ago that I was not cut out for serious handiwork I have come to rely on such people as David and my good friend Ron to step in and show me the way. I have often

had to ask Ron to show me the way, which he does so well, so often that, even before we notice it, he has finished the whole job before I have a chance to try my hand at each new skill.
But we each have our place in life. Mine is not to do important DIY jobs – it is to support those who do. I do a great job of fetching tools and making tea, and I try to keep my saviors supplied with other, sometimes more appreciated refreshments.
Andréas was proving to be another such friend. When I say just the sort of neighbor you need I should really say that he was just the sort of neighbor that we needed. He was capable, kind hearted, caring and generous. But more than all that he knew every property boundary by heart and – this is the really important bit – he understood the system of water rights. That means that he was one of the few people who actually knew how the water gets into our storage tank – and when.
In the southern Spanish sierras water is a precious commodity. Our house is only around an hour's drive from the southern most desert in Europe. And yet we were on the edge of some of the most productive fruit and vegetable growing areas around. Indeed we drive through the market gardens of Almería to reach the desert.
All around our small holding other property owners till and tend their fields, and in turn the land gives back the tastiest oranges, tomatoes, peppers and other fruit that I can remember tasting – or am I just overcome by the romance? Mind you I do object to our modern western habit of expecting fruit and vegetables to be available all year round. Not only that but the supermarket chains have got us convinced that they should also be the same shape size and color all year.
Don't you sometimes wonder why apples don't seem to taste as good as they did when we were children? Or why plums in the supermarkets never seem to be as good as the ones we used to pick from your Dad's tree at home? Well the answer is simple, because then we ate things that were in season. We had no other choice. But today, apart from the stalwarts of the local allotment society, we grow little or no produce ourselves, and buy fruit and vegetables that have been forced out of season and then picked un-ripe so that they can be flown half way round the world to be just under ripe when the local superstore shoves it on the shelves.
What Andréas grows, and what is on offer on the various local markets is ripe when it is picked. More to the point it has real flavor because it is ripened by the sun, not by some ripening

agent or by carefully controlling the temperatures in which it is stored and transported.
That first evening, despite tiredness taking hold, I was really pleased to see Andréas taking an interest and showing concern. I was also really touched when he welcomed us, because he did so by giving us a hug and shouting in my left ear "*hola hombré*". Andréas is a lovely man but I judge that he is normally quite reserved in his affections for relative strangers. As I settled into bed that night, exhausted and happy I turned to Kathy and whispered, "He called me *hombré*".

2 - "You can't call that a fig tree!"

Having visited a few old (and sometimes very run down) farmhouses around the area in search of our dream home, we commented to the agent on the charming names which so many of them had – *"Cortijo las Ramblas", "Cortijo Allegré", "Cortijo Sierras", "Cortijo Las Almendras"* etc. We told him how appealing these names were. "You see," he said "I'm not so stupid." The significance of that comment escaped us until he took us to see the house that we eventually bought. On reflection we had not noticed that none of these houses bore nameplates.

We met him for a coffee at 10 o'clock in a bar on the square and he and a colleague talked about the place we were off to see. Seems it was new on their books and he had not yet seen the property. The good news though was that neither had any other potential purchasers.

So as we drove up the drive to this property and liked what we saw we asked him what it was called. "Now let's see", he said, looking at the fig tree sapling just outside the front door. I would think "*Cortijo la Higuera*".

"Sorry, but what do you mean you would think?"

"Well you see none of these houses currently has a name. They're just known locally as 'The house where Juan lives' or 'The house where José lives' etc." In fact as he explained the property is all rather irrelevant, as it is the person that counts.

So the house now had a name - and a rather small fig tree to prove it. Some ten months later when the house was decorated and we started sleeping there we discovered that we had to give clear directions to the various additional workmen and delivery drivers. The gas, telephone and electricity men, the furniture company drivers etc all needed some clue to find us, and "The house that used to be Juan's" didn't seem to do the trick with all of them. I printed out a map and instructions in Spanish to show just where we were, but neither our name, nor that of the house was on display anywhere. So we decided that a bit of DIY was called for.

I bought the letters "LA HIGUERA" in Andalucían ceramic tiles. Although I'm not very handy I do have an independent streak at times, and occasionally I prefer to do some jobs myself, in the often mistaken belief that I do possess skills. So I bought the appropriate fixing cement and a couple of bits of wood to batten and fixed these tiles to the front wall of the unroofed storage area attached to the house. Of course I have little tiling experience, having left such jobs to others over the years, and was confronted by very uneven, rustic, stippled walls - a good three quarters of an inch difference in the surface at some points.

So now I had to attach these smooth tiles to this rough surface - and I was stubbornly determined to do so on my own, despite Kathy's plaintive suggestion that her father would love to do it. I didn't have to hit anything except a few pins to attach the battens - and that I did straight and level with little problem. The tiles though were a different matter, as their uneven facing for the next three months testified. Actually from a distance they looked just fine. After all they were in a straight line and level. They also did the job required of them by announcing to passing (and often lost) van drivers that this house is "La Higuera". That's pretty good really isn't it? But as you get closer, and as you run your hand over them it is not difficult to work out where the unevenness lies. The fact that some face southwest and some south-southwest is only really apparent when you get close. But I knew, and it niggled me every time I see them.

Visitors pointed out helpfully that had I put a layer of *cemento blanco* (white cement) on the wall first I could have created a smooth surface. I decided there and then that I'd bring a pot of white grout with me on the next trip and give the tiles a good smooth grouting - "hides a myriad of faults". I was then comforted with the view that the tilers had done a superb job of laying the floor tiles and tiling the various bathroom and kitchen walls - "not a nib in sight in the whole house". Yet in the 10 tiles, which I hung on that outside wall, there were at least a dozen "nibs".

That evening I went seeking the advice of Andréas on another, but related matter. We had no letterbox, and I had established that we did have a regular postal delivery - on condition that a post box existed in which the postman could drop our mail. We found out that his little white van has small piles of undelivered post on the floor at the back. He will try on various occasions to deliver, but eventually gives up – presumably when the pile reaches the stage of being a fire hazard.

So Kathy & I visited the local *ferretería* (hardware store) in Albox and purchased a smart black *buzón* (post box). We also bought a set of those self adhesive black on gold letters to spell out our name and the name of the house and off we went proudly to establish our presence with officialdom by providing a receptacle in which to deposit their demands, advises, invoices and notices.
I stuck the letters on the face of the box in what started off as a rather impressive arrangement. I was disappointed – though not entirely surprised – to discover that I had not left quite enough space for the name of the house in the flat face provided. The result is that the final "a" of "*Higuera*" runs at a slight angle. But it is clear to whom the box belongs. Even if it is not quite as smart as I had envisaged.
To make me feel better I held the box in my right hand, thumb over "a" and showed Kathy my handiwork. She was so impressed that she grabbed the article from my hand to have a closer praising look. Over the years Kathy has learned a degree of sympathy for my lack of DIY skills, and acknowledges that most of my problems result from my inherent drive to complete things. If only I took a little more time planning I would usually end up with a more polished result. But as I say she is sensitive to my feelings and simply said, "Well done" as she handed it back to me.
Having thus identified this post box as ours I needed to erect it prominently and it was in this connection that I went off to as Andréas for advice. On this visit our son Mark was with us and the two of us trotted off down the drive. We found Andréas picking fruit from his old fig tree and, as always, he greeted us like long lost friends – even though I had only finished a conversation with him a couple of hours earlier. He has a gruff voice, the voice of someone who has lived a hard life, but he always uses it effectively to demonstrate his seniority, and I always respect this.
I showed him my handiwork (thumb over the "a") and asked him where would be the best place to fix the box so that the *cartero* (the postman) would find it. He explained that these receptacles are grouped together so that the local *cartero* has fewer stops to make on his round. Our boxes it appeared were all together on a frame behind a couple of fruit trees opposite Andréas' house. He showed us just where it had to go, and rather than leave Mark and me to struggle as we made vain attempts at fixing this thing he took control of the situation immediately and attached it for us. He raided his workshop and found heavy-duty pliers and fencing wire, and thus equipped returned to the site to fix our

box for us. Somehow after this I felt that we were properly accepted. They'd see our post box and I had exposed to the whole village the poor standard of my DIY, and yet, somehow, I felt contented. I didn't feel any need to pretend with these people. This was a place where I could be a bodger and be content.

Andréas said nothing about the quality of my workmanship, and even as he later examined the house sign he commented on the choice of name - not the way in which I had attached the tiles. This could either be because he himself is a bit of a bodger at heart (after all he used twisted wire to attach our post box rather than self tapping screws - or whatever you should use) or because he was more concerned by the name.

Concerned is really a bit of an understatement. He handed over a bottle of his home made reddish wine and told me that he did not understand why we needed to give the house a name at all. After all everyone knew that this was the house where Juan used to live. But more serious than that - far more serious was his concern at "our" choice of name. It hardly seemed worth explaining that it was in fact Gordon, our agent, who named the property. And even if it had seemed worthwhile I wouldn't have got a word in.

Pointing to our tender young fig tree my neighbor explained at the top of his horse voice that "you can't call that a fig tree". "It is weak and bears no fruit," he told me. "It needs plenty of water." And "It will be some time before that becomes a proper fig tree". "That," he said, pointing at a magnificent specimen of his own, "is a fig tree".

I offered him a drink and, as always, he declined. I had not previously understood why, but this time he opened his shirt to show us the long scar, which resulted from open-heart surgery. He told us in gory details - in gory Spanish details - just what had been done to him. They had broken his rib cage replaced something or other and cleaned out something else. I felt my Spanish was coming along quite well really. Once I'd got the "somethings" sorted out there'd be no stopping me. Anyway he also explained that as a result of this obviously major bit of medical treatment he was no longer allowed to drink or smoke. So now I could guess at the cause of that gruff tone of voice.

A couple of miles or so away from us lived another English couple, Keith and Vicki. We met them on our first visit to the area as the agent proudly showed off one he had "prepared earlier". They were getting rather well established locally and that summer Keith and Vicki harvested their almonds and grapes as usual. Keith it was who saw an opportunity to save the exorbitant 150 pesetas a quart (around 90 cents) he paid for wine at the local bodega and decided to brew his own.

We have now seen and even tasted the finished result. He chose to give it to us in a sealed bottle to take away – almost as if he were ashamed of what we might say. He certainly had no cause for anything other than pride. The wine Keith produced was a fine medium dry white wine and excellent served chilled with salted almonds and olives. The wine that Andréas offered had none of that sophistication. It was cloudy, rough and had an underlying taste of the anisette that the bottles originally held! And he kept brining it!

Our neighbors are so good to us. Andréas would provide fruit and vegetables in season and asks for nothing in return. We have superb and tasty salads and Patricio and his wife, who lived between Andréas and us, gave us some succulent and tasty roasted peppers. You've heard the expression "I thought I'd died and gone to Heaven". All I can say is that if our Lord has made Heaven as friendly and as flavorsome as this then I for one could get used to the idea.

At the end of this particular trip in early September we started to say our farewells to the neighbors. We had hugs and kisses, and while no tears were shed I like to think that they were sorry to see us go. Andréas brother Pedro told us how important it was to them that we could speak enough Spanish to understand and to be understood. He told us how pleased they were that we made the effort, and he told us that he couldn't understand foreigners like that (pointing into the hills towards a house occupied by English only residents of the colonial type).

And Andréas parting shot was yet another go about the sickly little tree after which we had allowed our farmhouse to be named. I was just about to point out that we did in fact have another and far healthier fig tree at the top of one of our fields. But fortunately I held back, because as we went to get in the car Andréas promised to look after, water and nurture our little tree.

"And when you return in November you shall see what a fig tree should look like."

3 - Between here and there

Kathy and I both come from families with travel in the blood. Indeed her parents now live in the Spanish province of Alicante. Her father was a Royal Navy and later merchant sailor, and having left the navy his work as a printer's engineer took him to various parts of Europe installing equipment for Linotype. It's funny how things connect. David made several trips to Lyon and Paris - and gained a love of the latin way of life. He slipped easily into the work eat and play ethic of early starts and late finishes broken by a long lunch, made up of substantial and well prepared food and not insignificant quantities of local wine. I think a fair part of the extended lunch break was spent sleeping off the effects.

He even decided to repay his hosts on one follow up trip by setting up a bar in some part of the premises dispensing a selection of British drink. On his next visit after this his colleagues ushered him straight to one corner where table and chairs had been set up with a banner reading "British Bar". And who says the French have no sense of humor?

My parents and my mother in law were also adventurous - and between them had French, Russian and Danish ancestry.

As children we were both taken on vacation, when many of our school friends were left to entertain themselves, or even expected to help the family survive by doing housework or work in the fields. And while my neighbors went on vacation to Clacton or Walton, and Kathy's friends were in Blackpool or Llandudno our families took each of us on foreign adventures.

As children we both visited Ostend, Brugge and Brussels. My family went to Switzerland and Kathy's was amongst the first to sample the delights of an unspoiled Spain.

It is unsurprising then that by the time the two of us met we were both working in the travel industry. I was a sales manager in London and Kathy was in the reservations unit in Manchester, both working for Thomson Holidays. It was a new and very young company at that time, and one weekend a friend and I went to Estoril near Lisbon for the weekend. We returned to the hotel on our first day to be greeted by the "rep" who told me

that Norman Thomas, my counter-part from Manchester had been in that afternoon with a group of staff on an educational inspection trip. He left me a note that read "Eight girls, 2½ men. Party tonight. Hotel Tourismo. Please come and help".
What could I do? I was needed - and I could not let a colleague down. Company loyalty held sway and despite my own greater desire for a quiet evening in watching the fish tank I allowed my friend Paul to persuade me to go. After I'd twisted his arm that is. That evening Kathy and I met as she rescued me from a bit of a man-eater, and things developed from there.
That was in February 1973. Kathy went back to university in the September and thus it was that for the next couple of years we spent our weekends running about between Bournemouth and London and our family homes in Cheshire and Chelmsford. Over the years I seem to have spent a lot of my time between places.
My career has seen me with offices in France, Belgium, Spain and the UK - and often I would live out of a suitcase for days on end. In fact that first night in La Higuera was the start of the first consecutive 10-night stay in any one bed for eight months. And believe me I appreciated it.
On various vacations and business trips we have fallen in love with the location and known with certainty that at the time each was where we eventually wanted to settle. We would go off in search of estate agents. We would register with four or five and their details would arrive on our doormat for a few months. As they dried so we saw that our ideas had moved on.
We've made such forays to estate agents in Florida, Normandy, Brittany, the Lake District, Devon, Provence, Tuscany and other places. We even checked out the price of villas in Sri Lanka and apartments in Egypt. You can't say that our vacations do not leave an impression on us.
It was early in 1998, when work was especially frustrating, that we spent a week house sitting for David and Edith at their home south of Spain's Alicante while they were off cruising. During that trip we drove up to Castellon to visit long-standing friends who had retired to a small and still very Spanish resort. We were enchanted by the life and most impressed by the home, which they were extending in almond groves just a few hundred yards from the sea. After we said our farewells to our friends John and Judy we decided to visit a few estate agents. Well it makes a change - and we were encouraged by the prices that we saw. In fact at the time we could by an equivalent property for around 30% of the UK price.

On the afternoon drive back to Alicante we re-planned our future and decided to start preparing a prospective home in the sun within the next 18 months. We pawed over maps and weather data over the next few days and identified two possible areas. We knew that we wanted to find somewhere in the real Spain. Neither of us had any desire to live in a big resort like Benidorm. We love small village life and could not see any reason to settle for anything else. We also knew that if we moved into the hinterland and chose our location carefully we would be able to live comfortably, avoiding the oppressive heat and humidity that you tend to find on the coast.

So we settled on the *Jalon* Valley, an area in northern Alicante province, nearly at the border with Valencia, and the *Ebro* Valley, in Southern Catalonia. We decided not to rush - well that would be foolish - and also planned to see each at what might be the most uncomfortable time of the year - the *Ebro* in the chill of winter and the *Jalon* in the heat of summer. But not this summer. We would start in 1999.

Then two things happened. Firstly Edith came back to England in May for the funeral of a close friend. She brought with her a Spanish newspaper with an article by Howard, a friend of theirs, about the Almería region; and details of old and tumble down *cortijos* (farm houses) in that part of Spain, which she had found in an estate agency near to them.

The second event was that I had to attend an additional international board meeting on a Thursday late in August which our Spanish partner offered to host in Madrid. Kathy and I chatted and decided that as I was so close, and as we had a few frequent flyer miles she might as well fly out to join me for the weekend and we could "pop" down to have a look at Almería. That way we would see the hottest area of the three now on our list of options at the hottest time of the year. Madrid is not exactly round the corner from Almería. Spain is roughly three times the size of England, so such distances are not knocked off in a couple of hours. We ended up spending as much on flights from Madrid to Almería as we would have spent on charter flights from London - and gave ourselves only two days to get to know the area.

But we came away with a powerful impression. We saw the barren landscape marked by the plastic tunnels of the market gardeners, which looked like enormous reservoirs from the air. We saw the prolific agricultural part of the lower part of the Almanzora Valley in the north of the province and we saw the dry yet fertile conditions in the hills above the middle part of the valley, the area that was to become our second home. We saw the breathtaking views looking to the *Sierra de los Filabres* to the south, the *Sierra de las Estancias* to the North and the foothills of the *Sierra Nevada* to the west.

We also learned that this part is untypical of the region of Andalucía of which Almería is a part. Andalucía is not renowned for its good *Castilian,* the major language of modern Spain. And here they speak something more akin to *Murciana*, a sloppy and untidy version, which is spoken in the province of Murcia as well as here. Similarly there is none of the sophistication of the big cities of Andalucía. The central Almanzora Valley is between Andalucía and Murcia, but proud of its own heritage and history. Battles have been fought here and lives lost. Land has been won and lost and the culture today, though fiercely Catholic is influenced by the Moorish legacy.

It's a place like no other – somewhere between here and there.

4 - High in the hills

"La Higuera" sits on its hill overlooking the road into the village of Las Pocicas, which is around 2500 feet above sea level and 10 miles north of Albox, the nearest town. We are half way between the town and a religious sanctuary that commands the most spectacular views. This retreat is so grand that it is reputed to have as many windows and doors as there are days in the year. This number seems to have some mystical significance, and the building is somehow lost in time and distanced from the troubles of today.

It certainly is most impressive. The entrance to the chapel is through two magnificent carved wooden doors hung under a superb façade of local *travertino* stone blocks. Above this is a small stone tower with two window openings, giving the impression of a Mexican hacienda. The whole design is a mixture of the baroque and neo-classical styles.

The chapel, which is open to the public, is fairly small, but in excellent condition. It has a single aisle and a beautiful chancel before the high altar. To the left is a stone pulpit decorated with locally wrought ironwork, and the whole place offers tranquility valued by the locals. So many of us rush at and through life that we miss the chance to reflect and catch up with ourselves. For me a trip to this little haven provides exactly the right proportions of thrill on the drive up there and calm inside.

The entrance doors are really just the start when it comes to the woodwork here. All the doors and windows are impressively carved representing parables and bible stories or simple quotes from scripture. And all were produced by local craftsmen and by the resident members of the Church. In the past both the clergy and the local woodworkers would have labored on the land as well, to provide for their needs and to produce fruit and almonds that they could then barter for other things that they needed..

Like so many beautiful old buildings the sanctuary took a battering during the Spanish Civil War. Fortunately there has been a great deal of restoration work recently. The façade, the accommodation and the interior of the chapel itself are all fresher and more sound than just a few years ago. And that work

continues as extensive new building is underway in sympathy with the original design.
The sanctuary is around 5000 feet above sea level and nearly the highest point in the *Sierra de las Estancias* – the mountains that provide the views to our north. The province of Almería is bounded by mountain ranges to the north and west and by the Mediterranean to the south and east. The most famous range of mountains is the *Sierra Nevada* in Granada, where King Juan Carlos and his family ski each winter. To our south is the *Sierra de los Filabres*, ranging between two thousand five hundred and six thousand feet high.
The town of Albox is at the heart of the central section of the *Almanzora* Valley. It is also the seat of local government covering an area of some 1600 square miles, bounded to the East by *Arboleas*, by *Cantoria* to the South, *Partaloa* to the west and *Oria* and *El Taberno* to the north. Albox has a population of 10,000, and most of those people have grown up on or associated with the land. It is not a pretty town. The wealth was generated by marble quarrying and heading to the west the landscape bears the scars. Today one of its local claims to fame is that Albox is the driving test centre for a large part of northern Almería. The result is that the town seems to have more learner drivers than experienced drivers - and, based on the terrible driving around town you rather get the impression that the experienced ones managed to avoid taking the test.
I am sure that the Spanish are equally concerned, and possibly confused, by some of our driving habits, especially the "back before you can blink" tendency. They must find it quite confusing that we can set off apparently on a journey and return no more than a few minutes later, only to depart once more just minutes after that. A classic example was the afternoon one February when we set off for the airport, waving farewell to Andréas' brother, Pedro. We exited our main driveway and immediately turned back into the second lane, which leads to the back of the house. We knew that we had forgotten to lock away the 90-year-old pot that we had unearthed in clearing up the place. We always stand this outside the front door when we are in residence, but <u>always</u> lock it away again when we leave.
If that was confusing, Pedro didn't show it as we circled the house and exited a second time. Ten minutes later on the approach to the town Kathy asked me if I had emptied the fridge, and thus started a second return to the house, this time preceded by an emergency stop, a "U" turn and a few well chosen words. Pedro was not around as we drove in the back

way, and, having cleared away the few remaining lettuce leaves and the opened bottle of milk, we carried on to leave via the main driveway, in the full knowledge that this time we had not been spotted. But as we reached the bottom of the drive there sat Pedro, peeling a freshly picked orange and looking very concerned as he watched us wave adieu for the third time in half an hour. We didn't bother to explain.

For some time while the building work was underway we spent our nights in a hostel that the builder first booked for us. We stayed on and off in this small private hotel while our house had windows removed and walls plastered; floors ripped up and plumbing installed. *Hostal Rosario* is owned, managed and run by a hard working lady called Apollonia. She was always a very pleasant hostess, for whom nothing seemed too much trouble. The bar and dining room downstairs has two floors of bedrooms above – in total some 16 rooms. Not only does Apollonia run the place, as far as we could work it out she is the only employee. We have seen her serving at the bar as we fall up the stairs to bed at 2 in the morning. And we have seen her back on duty serving coffee and pastries at 7am. In our case though these two events were separated by several days.

She is always there to greet us with a kiss and a smile, she serves the drinks, cooks the food, serves in the dining room, cleans the bedrooms, changes the beds and washes the laundry. The building has no heating, and usually of course this is not important, frost is not very commont here. But when she has finished washing sheets and towels – by hand – she then hangs them out to dry on a first floor balcony. The balcony faces west and hence gets the late afternoon sun. And, as the hostal is built on the side of an escarpment,t it also gets a good breeze, so the washing has a good chance to dry.

Yet somehow the towels and sheets feel damp. And of course there is always the sense of detergent, because her rinsing technique seems to leave a bit to be desired. Heating is not one of Apollonia's priorities. The door to the bar is open at all hours and she just adds another layer of jumpers when she feels the chill. For her guests this is not always so easy, and also not always as effective. Her homemade soup helps, and failing that one of her generous glasses of brandy is always available. But at bedtime you still have to brace yourself as you slip between the quite chilly, slightly damp, rather stiff, washing powder scented sheets.

Apollonia's has a number of distinct advantages though. Certainly when we were staying there a double room cost just

3,500 pesetas a night – that's around $22! Usually we had a room with "facilities", only once did we have to creep along the corridor. We ate with Apollonia on several occasions, but, as you do, we tried to experience alternatives whenever we could. Her food was fairly basic, but was always well cooked and in generous proportions. The trick was not to be too fixed to one's expectations.

Apollonia tends not to worry too much about menus. She usually offers soup or a salad as a starter – whether the temperature is 40 degrees or 95 degrees. She leaves it to her guests to sort out the seasonal appropriateness. There will then be a fish option and a meat option, ragout perhaps or chicken. Having selected from this relatively short list of options we would wait to see what might arrive, for we learned early on that what we ordered had little or no bearing on what Apollonia served.

Anticipate deep red meat cooked in a heavy dark sauce and order a full bodied red wine to accompany it, and smile as a plate of lightly poached fish and a selection of fresh vegetables appears on the table. It seemed uncharitable to question her after the first time when she smiled her charming smile, said "Of course" and walked away.

After dinner there was always another surprise for the options were to sit in the bedroom with just one upright chair and on a cold night very little comfort or in the bar downstairs. Apollonia had obviously decided on a clean modern atmosphere. The whole place is clean but the bar is furnished with square pine tables and small-unpadded square pine stools. I am (just) a little on the large side, so I do have two particular challenges with these stools. The first is that the lack of padding means that my weight and the force of gravity ensure that I feel the hard surface very clearly. The second is that the seats of the stools have good solid square corners and a small surface area, ensuring that at a minimum of three points I get poked by the wood.

The bar has the added "attraction" that this where Apollonia watches TV – Spanish TV – very loud Spanish TV. Her favorite program is a loud and low budget game show. At least I think it's just one show. Kathy on the other hand thinks she watches six or seven different programs, which just happen to be indistinguishable from one another. She also enjoys an equally cheap production soap opera where everyone shouts a lot, most of them fall ill quite often, the set moves and the audience is clearly required to contribute by shouting back at the TV set and laughing uncontrollably.

Under Latin Skies

We were always grateful to be given a room at the back. We would be insulated from the road noise and the chatter, TV and shouting from the bar, and we could sit on the bed and look out through the smallish window to the views beyond. Because the hostal is high above the *rambla* (the dried river bed) below the views can be breathtaking, especially as the sun sets in a bright red sky behind the hills at the western edge of the town. The hills here provide wonderful views and exciting experiences and Apollonia's home, high on a hill, is no exception.

5 - Lawyers and Notaries

Cortijo La Higuera was not our first choice. It was the right choice though.
We had originally selected another old farmhouse further north near to the beautiful mediaeval town of Velez Rubio. The agent presumably named *Cortijo Oliverico* because it had olive trees around it. But I can't find the word "*oliverico*" in any Spanish dictionary. It could be the name of the original owners I suppose. More likely though someone took a potential buyer to look at it and when asked the name blurted out the first thing that came into his or her head.
This little farmhouse was no more really than a remote, but absolutely charming, farm cottage. It had been well cared for, but we doubted that it had been lived in for years. Just an outpost for someone tending the land around is my guess. Electricity had been connected fairly recently, but there was no plumbing and water came from a well at the entrance - that caught my imagination, and romance got in the way of logic.
We planned the terraces and the conversion, and even decided where the swimming pool would eventually go. We sorted out how we would arrange for the 8 acres of almond trees to be cared for, and we rather yearned after being miles from civilization. There are other smallholdings on the way and the lane is in fairly good condition - but the house is still 3 miles from the road. The views were the best we had seen on that trip - the other houses we were shown ranged from claustrophobic terraced bargains for a few thousand dollars to large swathes of land with a ruin.
Oliverico had enough land and was in passable condition. Never buy anywhere that has lost the roof we were advised. Water gets in and the masonry swells, creating unseen problems stored up for the future. This place had a good solid roof and the walls stood firm and true. The stables would be knocked down and two new bedrooms built in their place. The first floor, built to store grain and animal feed would be removed to create a wonderful high vaulted ceiling throughout the house and the tiny windows would be replaced with three foot square apertures to allow us to

relish the views. These Spanish mountain houses have small windows to keep the heat inside in winter and outside in summer. The realtor who showed us the house, could not understand why the British insist on putting in big windows. "To let in the light," we said. "To allow us to enjoy the views".
We generated all sorts of ideas - the back of the house might have large patio doors installed to allow the house to open onto the terrace and the 15 miles of uninterrupted views beyond; a swimming pool set below the terrace and so on. I think it was all too fast for our Spanish property salesman who was simply trying to give us ideas. His head hurt Kathy decided - he certainly rubbed it a lot. But he just accepted that we were crazy with a degree of resignation and watered the small vegetable garden, which grew fabulous peppers, tomatoes and rhubarb.
We left promising to get in touch to confirm our interest and trotted off to look at other properties. I was later that day that another agent took us to see Keith & Vicki's house and we first saw the village where we were eventually to end up. We saw the sense of living in a community. After all that was what we wanted to do, but the only house on offer there had little land, and that was across the road. This small terraced house was in good condition on a friendly little *plaza*, or square, but it was not what we were looking for.
The next day we contacted another agent who we were meant to meet nearby and told him not to bother. We reckoned we'd seen enough to form a reasoned view and decided to drive the two hours north to Kathy's parents and to relax around their swimming pool. We talked with them and went out for a quiet drink that evening on our own. We planned and re-planned what we could do with Cortijo Oliverico if we bought it and decided that if we bought anything from that trip this was the only choice.
Having met up in Madrid, in the centre of Spain, on the Thursday evening, Kathy and I were to part ways again in Barcelona – at the northeastern side of the country. You might think that we were set on making things hard for ourselves – and I have to say that you would be right. The problem was that having been in Madrid on business on the Thursday I had to be in France on the Monday. Add to that Kathy's need to be back at her office in England for work on the Monday and we were left with finding a pragmatic solution to achieve this. Flights from Barcelona seemed the only option. So we made our way there on Sunday and were ready for bed by around 8pm. But not before we spent

some long time going over the pros and cons of buying this remote little farmhouse, with which we had fallen in love.
Our next trip could not be before the end of October and we decided that if we were to go ahead with this we would need to keep the momentum up in our absence. Over a drink in our airport motel we decided to do it, and to listen to the advice that we had been given that we should use an English speaking law firm, because, after all, they would know what to do.
Thus it was at crack of the business day I was on the phone from an airport somewhere in Europe to tell the agent that we had decided to buy and would send a fax of confirmation on my return to the UK next day. I assumed, naively, that there would be no more to it. As time was to tell – I was wrong.
Back home I sent my fax of confirmation and advised the agent that we were appointing a London firm of solicitors who dealt in Spanish property law and who had offices in Spain. We had been told of the horrors of buying a house only to find that it has enormous debts attached to it – because in Spain mortgages and various other debts such as unpaid local authority rates are attached to the property rather than to the owner. We had also been told of the risks of buying through a private contract that is never actually in front of the notary. The notary is a civil servant, whose job it is to check that various contracts and the like are in order. But the Spanish are generally suspicious of officialdom and especially wary of any process, which requires them to divulge personal financial details to an agent of government. Thus many contracts are never formalized and numerous people live and die in properties that pass to their descendants despite the fact that the home has not been officially recorded as theirs.
We did not want to take such chances and hence followed up an advertisement in a property magazine for this London based firm. They had led me to believe that they had a partner local to our planned new home. As I was to discover the "local" factor was really rather a relative measure. He was certainly nearer than the London office. He was also nearer than the firm's Malaga office. But at over 2 hours drive away I would not consider this local and I regret that I did not do more questioning and checking. For example I wish that I had understood that things are done differently in different provinces, and that even some notaries do things differently to others.
Thus it was that we started several weeks of "blame-storming" and acrimony. The agent told us that without a contract he could not guarantee that another buyer might not snap up our dream, and the solicitor told us that the agent was un-cooperative. The

lawyer's Spanish partner (in London mind you) asked for various papers, including proof that there were no debts attached to the property. The agent faxed all the papers through, but made the point that under local convention it was their responsibility to hold these papers in their own keeping until completion of the sale. They invited the lawyer to visit their offices, as is normal practice. At the same time they suggested that the lawyer should complete the private contract that normally precedes the notarizing process locally. We went through the process of entering a power of attorney process to allow the solicitor to represent us. To achieve this we had to appear before a UK notary, who has a somewhat different role to his Spanish counterpart.

It was after completing this process that we realized that our lawyer's Spanish agent would have to travel for the best part of a day to do the job. And he could not do so immediately. So they entered a battle of telephone messages, mostly it seemed passed through me. The lawyer in London insisted that the agent forward the necessary papers immediately, while the agent insisted equally strongly that he was not allowed to do so.

And so it was at around 10pm on a Friday in early October that we received a fax from the agent to confirm that he had advised the lawyer earlier that day that "our" house had been sold to a third party who entered a private contract earlier that same day. Our lawyer had not chosen to tell us the news in person, preferring I guess to break the news some days later by post. I would suggest that this described the cause of our situation fairly well.

We had spent 6 weeks planning everything we could do to this house and had spent quite a bit on legal fees and communication. In the meantime we had been branded as troublemakers. So we decided to cut our losses and do things the Spanish way. It was that weekend that I called the realtor and asked if he had somewhere in a location similar to Keith and Vicki's house in Las Pocicas. He called again a few days later to say that he had just been offered this house on the edge of the village and that, bearing in mind the circumstances, he would promise not to put it on his books before Kathy and I had the chance to see it. I told him that we would be there three weeks later, and that was when we realized that loosing Cortijo Oliverico was good news.

David and Edith supported our view that La Higuera was right and we decided to go with the flow and enter a private contract. The realtor offered a choice of local "*abogados*" or solicitors. We chose the one who seemed to have the most experience of dealing with the British, a local office and enough English to get us through. We met him next day and he negotiated the contract with the agent until he was happy for us to sign it. A good Spanish realtor will already have checked the ownership or title of the property and will provide proof of this and proof that there are no debts attached to the house. This he did and the lawyer went carefully page-by-page through the papers in his office. He asked questions and requested various documents until he was satisfied, and he explained to us throughout what he was doing. Now I understood why our original legal firm and the agent found it so difficult to do business. They were from different cultures and their expectations were at variance with each other.

So we paid over a £1000 check as a deposit and headed off with a contract in our case and a great sense of satisfaction in our hearts. The next issue was the value to declare on the *escritura* the legal confirmation of sale. We wanted to declare the full value, and the seller wanted to declare the minimum to avoid giving too much away to officialdom. We had been advised before that the man who knows best about these things is the *notario*. He is the man whose advice would be sought in the event of any dispute, and it is to him that the taxman would turn if he felt that there had been any dodgy dealings. Our *abogado* gave the same advice and so it was that we let him persuade the vendor to take the same official line. He succeeded and early in December we finalized the details. We had hoped to stand in front of the notary in person to mark this chapter in our lives, but had to settle for giving our Spanish lawyer, power of attorney. This also requires notarizing, but could be done at our convenience. So we did get a brief moment of officialdom, following a two-hour wait in the notary's outer office. That same day the vendors sought us out to hand over a set of keys in person and then insisted that we walk round the property with them to check its condition. They and their family have become close friends as a result.

Legal advice takes many forms. One of the best moves made by the local council was the appointment of a foreign residents' adviser. Max, a resident Englishman did a super job of helping Brits and others through the wrangles and differences of setting up home in a foreign land. He was not paid a fortune, but regrettably following the 1999 local election, the incoming mayor was persuaded that others would do the job for nothing. It'll never last.

6 - It's "on offerta"

Not much seems be sold at full price in Spain - not much of any value anyway. We had often heard friends talk about buying clothes or furniture on *offerta*. I assumed that this was just a stock clearance system a bit like a department store sale at home. Or as it seems to have become, an excuse for selling specially bought in stock, which the store would not normally sell, at not very special prices. It is certainly true that stores in Spain have sale seasons under the *offerta* label, with banners across the windows and special price tags. They will thus clear end of season stock, or ends of lines. But in Spain *offerta* seems to mean so much more.

There is a residual culture of haggling here. It is not as extreme as the bargaining that is so prevalent in the souks of North Africa and the Middle East, but Spanish traders do enjoy a good negotiation - even if it is only over a garden pot or a chair. Our first *offerta* for our new house was negotiated not by us, but by our builder. It was late one December evening while we were planning the work to restore *La Higuera* and provide us with the dream house in the hills that we were looking for.

I had already drawn my view of the layout, and on several long November evenings back in the UK Kathy and I had played with it making various changes along the way. I would then take the latest plans with me as I traveled on business and fax back to her another suggested change. It was on a delayed flight from Geneva to London that I realized that we could substantially increase the size of the proposed new bathroom by simply knocking through into the rather over-generous scullery space and using part of that as an alcoved toilet cubicle. The following week I flashed back a further amendment, this time using that space as a very generous walk in shower cubicle, and placing the toilet where the shower had once been. In doing this we also created two impressive new built in cupboards, a linen cupboard in the bathroom and a display cabinet on the other side of the wall in the dining room.

The walk in shower is wonderful - no shortage of space and no access problems for us to face in our dotage. But the best thing about it is that we created a bathroom large enough to accommodate a decent sized bath and a feature washstand. So by the time we sat down with the architect we were clear about the general layout. As he was working things out on his office computer I uttered one of those throwaway lines that might normally be lost in time. But this was to be a pebble in a pond that created quite some ripples. I simply asked "I suppose a Jacuzzi bath would be out of the question?" and before Kathy had a chance to take in just what I had said he was on the phone and blasting away in full flow. He looked at us for re-assurance – but we were not at all sure what he was up to. We assumed that it had something to do with us, as he seemed to be including us in his thinking, looking at us and then at the latest version of the plans in turn.

After quite some chat, most of which seemed to be about their families and plans for a get together the following week, he changed tone to a more confidential, almost reverential manner. He eventually hung up and told me "It most certainly is not". "It most certainly is not what?" "It most certainly is not out of the question."

So we were playing twenty questions and I had completely lost the plot. It was Kathy who caught on first – "The spa bath you mean?" "Correct". It seemed that he had negotiated one on *offerta*. The result was that for "just" another 80,000 pesetas (or $500) we could have a corner bath that would make as many bubbles as you liked. At that point I was prompted to tell our designer about a training video which a colleague and I had made many years earlier to inform young travel agency staff about the joys of a brand new selection of villa vacations. We made this 10-minute piece in the form of the then famous Smith & Jones head to head sketches. As the (slightly) larger of the two I took the Mel Smith part, while Richard played Griff Rees Jones. At one point I explained that some of the villas even had Jacuzzis. "Jack what?" asked Richard. "Jacuzzis, you know baths that you can make bubbles in." "I don't need any special bath to make bubbles," replied Richard – un-scripted of course. We thought that it was hilarious at the time in time honored over-grown schoolboy style. The architect was polite enough to smile, but on reflection I don't blame him for not guffawing. He must have wondered by this time what he was getting into with us.

The following morning we met him at 10:30 as planned and no more than an hour and a half later, once he had sorted out the various other 10:30 appointments that he had apparently made, we were on our way to see this special offer bubble bath. He tends to use local suppliers, he wisely supports local businesses to the point where many of them have come to depend on him, giving him and hence his clients a fair degree of clout and a certain respect in the area. The sanitary fittings specialist also dealt in ceramic tiles, so I had to keep Kathy focused on the job in hand while we studied our new bath and confirmed that it was indeed what we wanted. Our new friend the architect then explained to the shopkeeper that we were really rather disappointed (although how he expected to be believed while we looked as pleased as punch I'll never know). The response was a free set of antique style taps for the bathroom - *un recuerdo* or gift, another regular factor in closing a sale.

Before we left we chose a super antique style wash stand - or vanitory unit, as estate agents in England seem intent on calling them. I presume that this is some estuarial English corruption of the word vanity, and I become increasingly frustrated by the distortion of the language. I am nowhere near as fanatical as the French in these matters, but Roger, my brother, has in the past threatened to sign me up as a member of the BPS (The British Pedants Society) - would that my own application of grammar were perfect. All in all that morning proved a very fruitful mission. We spent quite a bit of money that we had not earmarked for this purpose, but more to the point we had found the first two bargains for our house. We knew that they were bargains because the man in the shop told us so - in that "I don't know why I'm doing this to myself.... Wife and children to feed.... Food from their mouths" sort of a way.

Our project manager's local connections proved useful on numerous occasions. Had we been buying ceramic tiles in the UK we would probably have driven to "Tile em High" or some such large tiling retailer to be sure of finding a suitable selection of quality tiles without paying through the nose. Or so we thought. Back in that same little shop in rural Spain we were shown hundreds of different floor and wall tiles. And every one was top quality. We liked so many that choosing could have been difficult, but for the fact that we both preferred the same ranges. We started to worry when the shopkeeper took a particular interest in our choice of floor tile, a super handmade terracotta style with the most attractive border tiles. "These must be expensive," we agreed. And sure enough they were over our budget.

His allowance was 1,000 pesetas a square yard. That's only $6 and the tiles we had chosen were very special, so they would be bound to add significantly to the cost. But we were still thinking in British price terms, and we had forgotten the power of the *offerta*. These tiles eventually cost 1,600 pesetas a square yard, around $9.60. We found the self same tiles in our local British branch of "Tiles R Expensive" at $50 a square yard. Choosing the tiles we really wanted, rather than settling for the cheapest available added around $500 to the restoration bill, and once down they have helped to make the house very special.

So when we came to choosing an oven and hob we took the architect's advice and a copy of his business card and made our way to another local store, this one rather grandly titled *Hiper Ocio*. It has a wide selection of white and brown goods, garden furniture, several ghastly ornaments and a few impressive pieces, plus everything for the cyclist. The staff are friendly and the choice is good. But, by British standards, "hyper" it is not, and a good thing too I decided. We looked at various cooking equipment and settled on the bits that suited our needs - except that Kathy wanted the oven in white rather than brown, the only color on display.

The assistant (or was it the proprietor?) could not have been more helpful. And once she knew that we had been recommended things got even better. She assured us that she would find the white oven and arrange immediate delivery - no three-week wait over here. And she patiently explained that we qualified for the special price, because of that recommendation. This man's buying power worked even in his absence. Since then we have been back to this shop for several other bits and pieces and have always been impressed by their ability to supply just what we are looking for, and at prices to match the large discount stores in the big cities.

From these experiences we have learned not to take any price tag for granted in such shops locally and if everything else fails we could always ask whether they offer a special price for recommended customers I suppose.

I have always enjoyed bargaining. In Egypt I once negotiated a young lads price for the T-shirt he was selling down to 20% of the asking price. I actually gave him a second payment as a gift for "local advice", so he got a very good price from me, but we both had the satisfaction of a jolly good haggle. In the old souk in Istanbul I once went to buy a pack or Turkish delight as a present and did such a good job that I walked away with seven packs for the price originally offered by the stallholder. I was very pleased with myself, and he must have been satisfied or he would not have done the deal. The next problem was what to do with the extra six packs of Turkish delight!

David and Edith brought the boys to visit the house during the spring. Afterwards we all went back to their home further north and visited the evening market together. Mark and Paul have enjoyed the local craft market since they were small and, like their father, enjoy the thrill of a good bargain. One of the features of this market is the Senegalese chaps who sell everything from josticks and cheap electrical goods to carpets and carvings. Kathy and I were taken by the ebony carvings, and especially liked one of a couple holding a ball aloft. It was obviously deeply symbolic but of what I'm not entirely sure.
We were both stunned by it, and decided that it was just what we needed to stand in a low alcove which we had created by closing off a "bang your head" type doorway. We very nearly blew it all by showing our enthusiasm and had to walk away and casually saunter past a quarter of an hour later to start the process over again. The boys played their part, Paul saying, "You don't want that", and Mark asking, "When are we going?" We talked with the stallholder for sometime and eventually admitted that it could be attractive, but only if the price were right. Our offer crept up and his price nudged down. I said "Or perhaps this much smaller piece might do" and Kathy suggested that we leave it for another day.
Not surprisingly that sculpture now graces the alcove in our lounge and we had the builders add a down lighter to create the best effect. It needed a boost to lift it off the ground and show it off to best effect, but more of that later.
My enthusiasm has left me with several unwanted bargains over the years, including clothes that will never fit me, food that we will never eat, and even a small stockpile of saffron that I once bought really cheaply from a market trader in Luxor. And I've continued to make the same mistake here. We once had two pounds of superb *jamon serrano*, the local ham, bought as a real bargain as the market was closing one day. Unfortunately it was just a few hours before we left for the airport for business trips that did not take us directly home. Still it made interesting if unusual gifts for a few new friends. And of course it hadn't cost us a fortune to satisfy these near strangers because the ham was on *offerta*.

7 - Water, water

"So if water is so precious why is there a constant stream of it running along the side of the road?" We asked ourselves that question as we wondered at the quantity of water, apparently pointlessly rushing along the concrete channel which runs parallel to the road along the boundaries of the parched almond fields. As always here there is a sensible and well-tested explanation.

Water is greatly valued, and a downpour is seen as a blessing. For the people of the villages around us the rain that falls directly on their land is a bonus to be welcomed, even treasured. It is not though to be relied upon. In our first eight months here we have known just three serious spells of bad weather. When it rains though it drops by the truckload.

Long ago our new neighbors and their predecessors learned how to tame the water to their advantage and introduced several serious water management initiatives. The water, which they drink and use, travels several miles from the Sierra de las Estancias to satisfy the needs further down into the valley. And that water often hits the ground as snow, usually many months before. The snow falls for a few weeks each year high up in the hills and as it melts it passes through the topsoil to be filtered by the stone layers beneath and finds its way into the aquifers within the heavy layers of stone. There it settles or moves slowly until it finds its way further from its source to form small underground rivers that flow downhill deep within the mountain range. Mankind for longer than I care to imagine satisfying its needs has tapped these streams of hidden water. The snowmelt serves the local need for *agua* throughout the year, and those hills are extremely generous. Because our hamlet is only two villages down the hill from the peak, the water that satisfies our needs is in plentiful supply when it reaches us.

The situation in our village is fairly typical of the villages in the region. Water arrives at some properties in tankers the contents of which are then used to fill the individual water storage tanks.

Other houses, like Cortijo Oliverico, have private wells that tap the rich underground stocks.
Our house and those of our various neighbors has a different system. But first you need to understand that the water that is delivered to the house arrives by one of three different distribution systems. The water under the hills is tapped and delivered into the village, where it appears at a *fuente* or fountain on the other side of the *rambla*, the dried up river bed at the back of the parish church. There is appears from three rather cruddy looking pipes which poke out of a wall beneath a tiny glazed cupboard which contains a statue of the Madonna.
The water pours unrestricted into a trough below and from there local farmers encourage their goats and dogs to drink. But the water gushing from those open pipes is the purest and sweetest water I can remember. Here one fills containers for drinking water, and thanks to my mother and father in law we have a goodly supply of gallon water containers, which, once emptied by them, they have passed on to us to use for our domestic drinking water. The water that falls unclaimed finds its way into fairly large storage tanks, as big as a generous private swimming pool, to feed the second water system, the irrigation water.
The irrigation water passes along those channels that run alongside the road, and its content is very closely controlled. A number of locals will use this water for their ablutions, or even for their laundry, but for the most part this water is there to enrich the land. The Spanish have a well-earned reputation for being laid back and for a well-honed loathing of bureaucracy. But give them an opportunity like this and they will devise and respect a system so complicated that you need to be fourth generation to have any idea what it is all about.
At Easter Andréas found us in the town market, on the day we arrived with in-laws and sons, and explained at 120 decibels aimed carefully and directly at my "good" ear that he had entered our name in the village "water register". I was very impressed and Kathy's mum thought we must have done something really important. We had no idea what he was talking about, and at that point we still had no idea how the water system worked. Later that day we paid a visit to Keith and Vicki and explained this strange encounter with our neighbor, and they in turn explained the enormous significance of this.
It seems that just a few days earlier Andréas had rounded up Vicki and Keith and led them to one of the village elders – the ones responsible for the *agua*. There is a formal system of water management, the likes of which would make the major utilities

companies gasp in admiration, and at the same time suffer palpitations at the generosity of the system.
You see in addition to the drinking water at the spring and the irrigation water running freely down those channels there is a third supply of water. The domestic water is diverted from the *fuente* pipes and led to the storage tanks of private houses. Some incomers have wondered for weeks how the water gets into their water tanks, for they have been told that they do not have mains water. In some cases there is a bit of labor involved to haul heavy industrial strength rubber hoses between the stopcocks and the tanks. Indeed we know of one couple who found their hose curled up in a cave, which they were clearing out to use for storage. They were in the process of loading it into the trailer to dispose of it when a neighbor came running at full pelt shouting to them not to do it. It seemed that this was vital equipment and for some months he had been filling their tank for them in conjunction with filling his owns.
We are very modern by contrast, because our water arrives through black piping buried underground from wherever it originates directly into our tank. Well not exactly directly, that would obviously be a bit easy. Both the agricultural water and the domestic water are very carefully controlled. Each registered user is entitled to water for a defined time. In the case of the water for the fields, and assuming he is entitled, the landowner may open the sluice, which lets the water onto his land, but only at the time allotted. At the designated finish time he must shut the gate if he has not already done so.
A similar system operates for the water delivered to the house. Now forgive me if I am just a bit inaccurate in this description. This is entirely due to the fact that I have as yet failed to understand it. You see it's like this. Every 18 days in summer and every 24 days in winter (or is that the other way around?) each registered resident is entitled to draw enough water to fill his domestic storage tank. Well actually he is allowed to draw water for a designated number of minutes for the purpose of filling his tank. Thus if his tank is full, or if the end of his allotted time comes before the tank is full, he must stop. The system is so scrupulously fair that it divides the time available exactly by the number of residents entitled to take part. Thus it is that one's access time might start not at 8:30 am, but at 8:27 exactly – not a minute before. And if Andréas is in control not a minute after. The resident before one on the list would have switched off his supply before the moment arrive, because he would have

known that his supply must be completed before the minute at which his neighbor's would start.

We lucky foreigners have an Andréas to take control. Fortunately he enjoys taking control of the situation, because on some days the start time might be in the middle of the night – now that is a good neighbor, don't you agree. So it was that another British couple who moved into a village with a similar arrangement not far from us woke up at 3:30 to the sound of movement and the smell of tobacco smoke mixed with male perspiration. Assuming that the intruder was up to no good, they walked towards the aromas and the strange water like sounds. The husband tripped over an unexpected hose, lost in the dark because of its black color. He lost his balance and ended up with one foot in the opening of the water tank alongside the filler pipe and the other out behind him ballerina splits style.

His agony, embarrassment, sleepiness and not inconsiderable confusion were not helped by the voice of Fernando his kindly neighbor who said something along the lines of "I don't think you wanted to do that". This was followed by "And there was me thinking that you forgotten that your water starts at 3:23 in the morning. You are late, but at least you did not completely forget. Shall I leave you to finish off yourself then?"

Their position was not helped by the fact that their water tank had provided the foundations for a new kitchen, and the filler cover was in an "unobtrusive" spot slap bang in the middle of the kitchen. Our tank is outside, beneath what is now a delightful patio, and Andréas has never been so foolhardy as to think that I might have any intention of getting to understand the system. He is the expert and I would never want to deprive him of that exalted status. I have watched him at work, and because of our fully plumbed in model it is certainly easier than heaving out a great big three inch diameter hose in the middle of the night when decent folks are all abed.

Our part of the system is controlled by a sophisticated series of stopcocks. As with the rest of the village someone who is obviously in great authority controls the main water flow to ensure that the pipe leading to our stopcock is open when our time arrives. Our neighbor, Patricio, and we draw off the same connection. Because we are neighbors and because we get on so well together and so on – oh OK I admit I don't really know why, but for some obviously important reason we are allowed to have both his stopcock and mine open at the same time. There are a number of advantages to this (I assume) but it seems to me that the biggest advantage is that if he's not been to stay for a while and hence used very little water we can have a couple of extra therapeutic baths free.

Now don't go getting the wrong idea. I would not steal Patricio's water. In fact I don't have to, because neither he and his wife, nor Kathy and I have to pay a peseta for what seems to be a more than adequate supply of the clear fresh liquid. We are part of the lucky few. Some foreigners moving in to sunny spots will be charged a high price and be heavily restricted on the quantity available. Indeed some unscrupulous builders have been known to build several tens of vacation or retirement homes in drought areas, where water is either rationed or simply unavailable except by very expensive special delivery. Presumably they then set their younger brothers up in business as water factors.

The whole point of Andréas' gruff monologue in the market square was to let me know that he had arranged for Kathy and me, his *hombrés,* to be entered in the water book. This book was started shortly after the end of the First World War and provides quite an interesting archive of village life, listing the inheritances of numerous properties and the comings and goings of owners at others. It also confers on those whose names it contains the right to water - free and for life. In a climate like this that facility is worth the weight of the enormous ledger in gold.

Patricio cleverly constructed his water tank in one of his fields around 20 feet higher than their house. *La Higuera* is built at the top of our land so we cannot take advantage of gravity to deliver the water to the taps. Instead we require a pump. When we bought the house a rather small electric pump had to be switched on occasionally to fill a header tank sitting rather prominently on the apex of the roof. We decided to do away with the tank and instead to fit an automatic in-line pump. The result is a constant flow of water and the loss of the ugly tank.

The main disadvantage is that when the power is off there is no water. I first realized this at the airport on our way home. As our flight was called and we left Spain for 11 weeks I had this eureka flash of realization, as I comprehended the foolishness of my actions - yet again. It was the day when Andréas had told me that our fig tree would be transformed in time for our next visit. At his request I had left a hosepipe connected to the outside tap, and had carefully switched off the electricity as we left. Those two acts had the automatic effect of the latter canceling out the benefit of the former. No water and hence no *higuera*.

8 - Brick by Brick

Having committed ourselves to La Higuera in October a team of builders was ready to start work on the house at the end of January. In various conversations the proprietor gave us a range of completion dates. These included a clearly unconsidered suggestion that the work would be finished by the end of March. After thinking the matter through more carefully he told us that the structural work would be concluded by late May.

He is a lovely chap but inclined to make rash suggestions in a way that they can be taken by others as firm commitments. This is a trait of builders the world over and we learned a long time ago to ask the same question several times and push gently and frequently until things move forward in a sensible way. I remember meeting a couple at Barcelona airport some years ago. They were flying back to the UK in disgust because the work that they had paid for months earlier had not been finished. I asked how often they had checked on progress and it turned out that they had put blind faith in a nice chap they had met only days before. He had shown them a building plot and drawn up a private contract for them to sign. It said that they were buying the land and that he would build a house on it for them.

Naively they had handed over the price of the land and the twelve million pesetas (over $75,000) he quoted to build a house. They had selected a design from his book and he had said that he estimated 4 months for completion. So being trusting Brits they had gone off to the airport in a sense of excitement. They had then spent 4 months anticipating their new house, but had not thought it relevant to check on progress.

The builder meanwhile banked the money and was diverted by a subsequent client who put him under pressure to undertake another project. He knew that this couple were rather relaxed about the whole thing and of course they had not agreed any details of internal layout etc

"Knowing" that their new house was awaiting them they planned to hire a truck to move furniture over at the end of the 4 months, but the wife realized that they had not discussed decorating (let alone kitchen and sanitary fittings). So she thought it might be wise to see the house complete before bringing their chattels with them. They had the sense to drop the builder a line to let him know when they were arriving. He assumed that they would want to agree a plan for the works, both the detailed plans for the house and a construction schedule.

They arrived at Barcelona airport, picked up the hire car and drove straight off to their new home. They thought that the house would probably still look a bit like a building site. They had even considered that the windows might not yet have been glazed. But the one situation for which they were totally unprepared was a plot of land looking completely unchanged from their previous visit. Not a sod had been turned. Not a bag of concrete had been delivered. They had driven around the corner expecting to see an almost completed villa, and saw instead a building plot. I foolishly asked why they hadn't called the builder between times to check progress or even to ensure that they and the builder shared a common understanding of what would happen.

They had stormed into the builder's office to be greeted warmly by him in his expectation that now they could plan the work. They went to the local police station to report fraud. They then went to an English speaking solicitor who explained that as yet the land was not registered in their name, and that their "contract" was really no more than a general statement of intent its value was only as a receipt for money paid. Their faith was severely dented and they decided to cut their losses. So they sold the land back to the builder and he returned their money. Next day they found a card in his window advertising the land at 3 million pesetas ($18,000) more than they had paid for it.

They were not happy bunnies by the time I met up with them. They had lost their dream house – the dream that they had shared with so many friends and family at home. They had paid interest on the funds that they had borrowed to buy the land and fund the building. The builder had earned interest on those same funds for the last four months, and to top it all the land had appreciated in value and they had not benefited from that increase.

I was surprised that anyone could be that green, but was later to hear stories of countless trusting souls who saw their money go west. We were not to be caught the same way. We decided right from the start that everything would be put in writing, and agreed that with our developers. As standard practice they produce a detailed costing for each job, which both builder and client sign as their commitment to one another. We told them that we would be in regular touch with them and agreed that we would confirm every agreement along the way, whether they did or not.

We used e-mail and fax as well as phone and have kept in touch with them at least once a week since the process began. This way we have known the progress all along the way and kept ourselves at the front of his mind. To be frank I am quite sure that they have cursed modern communication on more than one occasion following a call fax or e-mail from us. The project manager did joke (I think) once that he might paper our walls with faxes from me! But we have had no major disappointments with him. The main structural work was indeed completed by May and we saw the final plastering and the start of the decorating when we arrived at the end of the month.

The architect had said that work would start before the end of January. On 8th January Kathy called me in Brussels to say that he had just phoned to say that subject to the weather holding out so they could complete another job they would be starting our work the following Monday. If the weather closed in they would start our house immediately and return to finish off the other project as and when the conditions permitted.

On the evening in December when we agreed the plans and costing for the project we were introduced to Pepé, the foreman on our job. He was to become a friend and a regular visitor. I was surprised just how much work was involved. The house was solid and in my mind we were only moving a few walls. As we visited over the following months we learned just how much they had to do, and became increasingly worried about the effect of everything they had to do on our four million peseta ($25,000) budget.

Each time we visited we called in to see them to review progress against the timetable and the budget. Each time there was an additional cost for some item of work or other, but each time there was a saving of some sort that would offset most if not all of that extra cost. At the end of the job the work, with all the various adjustments, cost almost exactly the agreed sum. The only extras were of our own choosing, the cost of the more expensive tiles, or the therapy bath.

In its "raw" state the house was around 2000 square feet, a cottage made up of eight rooms, each approximately 12 feet square. There was a spinal wall running the length of the house and the rooms were arranged four on either side. At the end of the house was a stable come garage and in front a rather poorly constructed walled storage structure without a roof. In fact there obviously had once been a roof. We could tell by the rust stains running down the wall. It did not take Sherlock Holmes to work out that sheets of corrugated iron had once protected it from the elements.

As I have said we thought of various possible plans, but throughout opening it up was at the front of our minds. The eight rooms consisted of four bedrooms, a kitchen a small snug and dining area created by opening a large archway between two rooms, and a sort of agricultural store room in which they had built a breeze block shower room and toilet. Walls please note that reached up to six feet and no higher – just high enough for privacy.

The feature that grabbed our attention most was the wonderful roof beams. With a few exceptions these were irregular trunks of old almond trees. In the exceptions more modern concrete or planed timber beams had been used to replace original beams that had rotted. We wanted not only to keep these beams, but also to make them the central feature of the house. Some had been painted, others varnished, others whitewashed and the rest left untouched. When we started we had no idea how we would achieve the blending of them together, because once whitewashed they could not be painted and once varnished they could not be whitewashed.

It was when I called our architect at the end of January to ask how things were going that he first told me there was nothing to worry about. This became a regular pacifier and always encouraged me to probe further. It also became a private joke between Kathy and me. When I telephoned in the evenings she might tell me that he had called and that fortunately there was "nothing to worry about". Or I would e-mail her after talking to him to let her know the good news "there's nothing to worry about!" I expect that Bill Clinton could have done with the same degree of certainty during his impeachment proceedings, or Churchill during the Battle of Britain.

But of course he was right. Worry would not have got us anywhere. It was a useful tool to focus the mind occasionally and consider options and solutions. At the same time as telling us that there was nothing to worry about he also gave us a fairly comprehensive blow by blow update on progress. We would then check how things looked to the neighbors and even asked David and Edith to pop down once or twice to establish that it was all up to our expectations. Between visits we received e-mailed photos of progress and we were as much in control of the situation as it was possible to be. Our expectations were well managed and on almost every visit we were pleasantly surprised by the progress that had been made.

We eventually settled on our final layout. This turned three rooms at the back into the new kitchen, the scullery, second toilet and the bathroom. The other two bedrooms were to stay, but only after we had them extended by several feet. The remaining three small rooms at the front of the house were all to be knocked into a 35 foot long dining hallway. And to complete this phase of the work the stable/garage, which 25 feet by 12, was to be converted into a new living room at the end of the dining room.

I had not realized that to lay pluming and wiring the floor had to be excavated several inches throughout the house. The end result though is outstanding as we now have smooth floors and all the electrical, plumbing and sanitary work is as hidden from view as it would be in a new house.

I was shocked though by the state of the house on our visit at the end of February. Everything had happened at once. Most of the internal walls had been knocked down, knocked through or moved. There was soil for flooring, and we had to step down rather than up into the house. Pepé was laboring away with a couple of other builders, but most of what they were doing seemed bent more on destruction than on construction. As my old granny would probably have said "You can't make an omelet without breaking a few eggs". I say probably because both my grandmothers and one grandfather were long gone before I was even born. So I really have no idea what either "granny" might have said. But you know what I mean I'm sure.

By the time we revisited with the boys and Kathy's parents at Easter things had swung distinctly into the re-construction phase. The floors were still not there, but we could see the course of every electrical cable, water pipe and soil pipe. And we had a final opportunity to add to or change the wiring of the house. We agreed with Pepé that an additional light was needed and added a few power points. This we were able to do at minimal extra cost because we caught the work at a good time.

As we left we were assured that the structural work would be finished by the time we returned at the end of May. How I simply could not imagine, and indeed I resigned myself to the idea that we would be disappointed on our next visit. But I was wrong, because from the moment we left Pepé and co. worked like Trojans, laying floors and tiles, re-building internal walls brick by brick and cementing and plastering to give the house the form that we expected.

9 - Marmoles

I came to read several tour guides on the area. Every guidebook on Andalucía talks at great length about the wonders of the great cities, Granada, Cordoba and Seville. They explain the importance of the "strip" along the Costa del Sol, saying on the one hand how important tourism is to the economy, and on the other how the glitz and pizzazz of the tourist meccas is untypical of the real Spain, which lies behind.

Many of the guides stop there. OK so there is reference to Jerez and the fortified wines for which the region is so famous. Or maybe they refer to the beauty of Ronda set high across the gorge in the mountains behind Estepona. Perhaps they talk about Mijas "a pretty white commune set high above Fuengirola". Or so says one guidebook. The fact that Mijas is now overrun by foreign money and extended in every direction up, down, north and south, to the point where the original village community has been swamped by tourism tends to be ignored. I remember visiting Mijas in the 1970s and wondering at the view. But even then the square was full of tour buses and a super international hotel occupied the best spot. Today it is difficult to find a Spanish speaker in Mijas. But the books tend not to tell you that.

There are exceptions of course, but the truth is that to do justice to a region the size of Andalucía in one book is difficult. This would explain why the province of Almería gets such a rough ride in these books. For some publishers the province does not exist. It's as if the author was ashamed of this rural desert area, and preferred not to mention it for fear of suggesting that the sophisticated southwestern provinces might somehow be tainted.

A few books are more adventurous. They will discuss the quieter resort areas of Mojacar or Roquetas de Mar. They will explain that these less sophisticated resorts might suit the visitor seeking a quieter less hassled vacation.

Some even mention the national parklands of the Cabo de Gata, or the Wild West scenery of the Almería hinterland. But just two that I found made any more than passing reference to the northern part of the province. In the others the references tend to be rather off hand, and concentrate on the lack of tourist attractions. You have to look hard to find books that might excite you to visit this area.

As a resident this is no bad thing, because I don't particularly want what has happened to parts of Provence or Tuscany to happen here. I really would not want to be overrun by 4by4 toting Sloanes with nannies in tow. The sort who try desperately to juggle the assets of their high flying employers on mobile phones and modems, while the children are left in the hands of others, on the "occasionally visible, but certainly not audible" principle. I do not want my bit of heaven spoiled by people who want spotlessly clean and totally "authentic" *tapas* bars run by some overrated chef or owned by "TapasYouLike" or similar. Kathy and I chose to live in rural Spain because we wanted to live in rural Spain. We did not want to end up in Manhattan by the almond groves.

Even so I was disappointed that so many eminent guides gave but passing reference to this part of Spain. The abiding theme seemed to be that the lower valley is green and fertile, with a good choice of habitable caves to visit. The upper valley moves into mountain scenery as the visitor approaches the foothills of the Sierra Nevada. But the central valley gets cold shrift from these eminent authors. They refer to the marble dust, which covers the countryside. And if you look only from the main road, the N336, to Baza you might form the same impression. But turn left or right for a few hundred yards and in most parts the quarries disappear. There is one spectacular drive over the hills from Macael towards Sorbas where precarious quarries are set on either side of the gorge and you have to wonder how on earth the peasant forebears of the people of Almería were able to work at such acute angles. And more to the point how on earth did they ever manage to transport the result to the workshops or the end users.

Marble has long been a vital mainstay of the local economy. It employs many of the areas men folk and it trains some of the country's most able craftsmen. The marble dust does appear in some parts, but so too do some impressive showrooms offering for sale beautifully carved and delicately crafted pieces of furniture or architectural stoneware. There are inexpensive marble tiles, marble lamps, worktops, tabletops, stairways and almost everything else imaginable. All are created from chunks of stone hewn from the local hills and shaped and reshaped by the hands of local craftsmen.

This area also produces other stone. The floors throughout the impressive new terminal building at Barcelona airport are built not from marble, but from a local stone, called *travertino*, which glories in the softness of its texture and the faults which mark it throughout. The main squares in several local towns are laid with the same stone, creating outstanding features of the fountain and the steps. Here young and old alike will rest from the labor of walking in the heat, or meet together for a chat, followed perhaps by a *paseo* in the cool of the evening. This stone does not have the durability of marble, but it is a less risky product to excavate, it is far easier to cut and mould, and it is found in large quantities in the hills of the area.

The *marmoles* industry is critical and be in no doubt if Spain and the World were to stop building cathedrals, hotels, private hospitals and airports this would be a poorer region by far. We chose marble worktops for our kitchen and the scullery, and were amazed that this was going to cost less than a similar area of laminated worktops had cost us in Hampshire several years ago. It was carefully fitted by people who obviously know what they are doing, and as it starts to mark with use it is developing a unique character that no manmade surface could achieve.

I was interested to find out that one of the first houses we looked at in our search for a dream house was owned by absentee owners who lived in Barcelona. It just seemed such a long way to pop down for the weekend. I was confused when we were told that the house had been in the same family for over a century. Obviously one local lad had broken loose and gone off to seek his fortune up north in the big city. Then we were confronted by the strangest coincidence, because the third house we saw had just been inherited by a family living in Barcelona. Not in Madrid, nor in Valencia, but Barcelona.

We came up with the answer. It was quite possible that the daughter of one family had run off with the son of the other. They were probably black sheep who had been welcomed back into the fold like the prodigal son. Now unfortunately both sets of parents had passed on to the great marble quarry in the sky and, well frankly, they didn't really need two weekend cottages so far away. Obviously they would have kept his parents house when they passed away to keep a link with her parents. But once her father and later her mother eventually kicked their clogs there was nothing to bring them back to the area so they might as well sell both houses and invest the money in a nice little beach house on the Costa Dorada. I was amazed that we could have thought this through so thoroughly, and a pretty good explanation it was too.

Under Latin Skies

The validity of this explanation became questionable though when we discovered an envelope in house number four from the Banco de Sabadell. I know this bank rather well as I have passed through the portals of their London offices on numerous occasions for business. I came to know that Sabadell lies a few miles inland to the north of Barcelona. So what was the explanation? I was becoming obsessed by this question when I noticed that we kept passing little white vans stuffed full of sacks of almonds on their way to somewhere or other – and every other van had a Barcelona registration.

I mentioned this to the estate agent in whose car we were travelling. The response from him was "oh really". Now don't tell me that I was the only one who had noticed the connection. Perhaps there was some mafia link – "would we get out alive?" Or maybe the Catalans were taking control of Spain in a sort of pincer movement, squeezing the country simultaneously from north and south. As always though the explanation came only once I had stopped looking for it, and it was nowhere near as dramatic as my own imaginings.

On the day that Juan and Francesca placed the keys to our farmhouse in my hand I saw once again the sinister link with the north rear its head. For the keys were on a key fob, which was obviously a business promotional gift – from "Marmoles de Sabadell"! So was marble the link? It seems that the skills developed in the Almanzora were highly valued, especially in the 60s and 70s, and as the job became more mechanized and less skilled workers were required. So other marble businesses were looking for just the sort of skills which these environs had in plentiful supply. So it was that many young families headed north to find their fortune. Fortune is a relative measure of course, but in comparison to the life style to be had in Almería the riches of sophisticated Catalonia were too much to resist.

Most of them stayed there, bringing up their children as good Spaniards under the closing days of Franco's regime. Latterly though as regional personalities were allowed to flourish once more, those children and their offspring developed into Catalans, and as always with migrants the ties with "home" started to weaken.

Thus those family homes are now becoming available at attractive prices as the families established around the Catalan capital let go their links with the homeland. And the little white vans? Well there is an even simpler explanation for this. It seems that the big cities require many small nippy light commercial vehicles for everyday delivery work and the like. In keeping with the demands of modern business these vans would be replaced while they are still in good condition. This means that there is a good supply of reliable little vans available at attractive prices, and hence smallholders will buy them and give them a whole new existence in the fields and byways of the countryside. They could have come from any of the big cities, but here, for some reason, some enterprising trader has established a link with Barcelona. And why are they all white? Well my guess is probably no better than yours. The best reason I can think of is that white reflects the heat of the sun, just as it does with cricket whites (well it does on the rare occasions that the sun shines on an English cricket square).

Having chosen our Senegalese wood carving to sit in the alcove, the one which gave so much pleasure in its purchase, we had to find a piece of stone on which to stand it to allow it to sit more comfortably in its allotted space. On advice we visited the *marmoles* factory at the Arboleas junction on the main valley road. We were trying to buy this piece of marble in late August when most businesses were only just re-awakening after the summer *vacaciones.* The man we met there was charming and offered to produce just what we were looking for in a few weeks time. That didn't fit our (admittedly very impatient) timetable. So we decided to leave it. But as we were leaving we saw two spectacular pillars. They were identical and each was constructed from several blocks of stone and marble laid in a spiral pattern to create the impression of being twisted. Each was designed as a central stand for a round glass top table, but we decided that with both pillars we could create an impressive rectangular table to seat eight or ten – almost exactly what Kathy had been looking for in various fashionable furniture shops. We talked about price and agreed a ridiculous *precio offerta* of 40,000 pesetas ($250) and he agreed to deliver that evening.

He sent us off to *Christaleria Garcia* to have a piece of glass cut to sit atop these supports and by 10pm that day we had a unique dining table which had cost us little more that $400. And the local industry, the *marmoles,* was exhibiting to every visitor to our home. No one could miss this masterpiece, which greets all comers as they enter through the front door.

10 - We could be famous

When we sat with our architect in his office one winter's evening working through options for our house I explained that we planned to video the work in its various stages, from raw state to finished perfection. We established that we had compatible video cameras and our conversation diverted into the possibilities for communication. Kathy suggested that he get some TV company interested in a sort of Spanish "New Yankee Workshop" series to promote the idea of restoration.

That weekend we had again traveled via Madrid. I had flown in from my Brussels office and Kathy flew on frequent flyer miles. We met up at Madrid and spent the night nearby with friends. The 7:30 next morning to Alicante was nearly empty and by the time we had picked up our little hire car and were on our way south at 9am we were wide-awake and ready for action. The return to Madrid saw us less fresh. It was Monday evening and we both had to be at our places of work first thing on Tuesday. We returned via Madrid to make best use of Kathy's British Airways ticket and my bargain flight with Virgin Express.

We had arranged for a digital satellite TV system to be installed back in England while we were away, and Mark phoned while Kathy was checking in to tell us that the engineer could not complete the installation that day because of an issue with the quality of our telephone line. Mark arranged to rectify this and when we arrived home, we sat down together to watch our first dose of digital TV. The choice is amazing, but I can't really say the same for the quality. That first evening we flicked through the forty plus channels that our $17 a month provided and we came upon an interesting program about a TV producer and his partner who were "doing up" a house in rural Burgundy. We really enjoyed this because like Alan and Rosemary we had considered Burgundy at one point as a possible future home, and as we got into it we realized that they were going through a process very similar to the one ahead of us.

A few days later the architect mentioned that he had been approached out of the blue by a TV production company interested in making a series about British living in the "real" Spain. I'm always a little unsure of people who talk about "real" Spain. The truth is that all of Spain is real. It's just that a very small part of it is not very Spanish these days. You might imagine people talking about visiting the real England because they avoid Blackpool. Of course Blackpool has created its own image of English seaside life, but it is just as English as cream tea or a country pub. Its provenance may not stretch back quite as far as some aspects of the culture but English it is through and through.

You have to look hard on a map to find Benidorm and Torremolinos, because there is so much more of the "real" Spain and the major cities stand out far more prominently. Those cities are also very impressive. In fact to me Barcelona is the most wonderful city in Europe. Paris is impressive, I know, with the wide boulevards and regimented architecture and Rome is spectacular in that you can walk amongst so much history, see it and touch it. But Barcelona is my kind of city. Like Brussels it is of a manageable size, but unlike Brussels it is clean, well cared for and its people take pride in their city. They don't spend their time letting dogs mess on the pavement and apologizing for the inadequacies of their city and indeed their whole country.

I do know what the "real Spainers" mean of course. As I've already said Kathy and I had no desire to end up in one of the big resorts. I wouldn't want to live in the real Blackpool without the sun, so I don't find the idea of a replica with sun a great deal more attractive. But just as the splendors of the Lake District and the more genteel lifestyle of Lytham and Fleetwood surround Blackpool, so Benidorm and Lloret are close to beautiful countryside and cultural attractions. And of course we had purposely chosen somewhere far away from that "all day English breakfast" version of Spain – philosophically far away if not geographically so.

We told him that if this TV business came to anything we would "of course" be happy to take part, and that we would be quite prepared to give an honest assessment of the process of buying and restoring our house. This seemed like a clever little encouragement to not leave us disappointed, but he's probably not very worried by such subtleties. I think he just carried on as normal. We heard no more, and apparently neither did he. I continued to do my Steven Spielberg bit, recording a few minutes of very amateurish video each time we visited to keep a memory of the remarkable changes that our house went through.

Under Latin Skies

The a few days before we were due to travel out in May Hazel, my secretary, told me that a foreign lady from Send It TV had been on the phone wanting to talk about our house. She called again, this time on my mobile phone, and we spoke through the crackles and silences of poor reception. It seemed that Send It TV had been put on to us by our man in Spain who knew that we might be prepared for our house to be featured on their planned TV series. I asked her what was planned and she explained a concept very similar to Alan Ravenscroft's "House in France" which we had discovered by chance on that first night's viewing of our new digital television system. When I asked it this would be similar she said, "That's right. We want to repeat the success of our "House in France" series." It was only then that I realized that she worked not for Send It TV but for Zenith TV. It really was a very bad line, so it's probably no surprise that I misunderstood.

We chatted for a while about what she was looking for. When I understood that they wanted to film a restoration project from start to finish I had to explain that our project was almost certainly too far advanced for their needs and we agreed to leave it at that. I did say though that if they would like to visit the house they would be most welcome. We discovered later that they did indeed reconnoiter our property, but we heard no more. It seemed that our moment of fame was not to be. That weekend I filmed the current state of the works and we left to call in on David and Edith and to relax around their pool for a couple of days.

The subject of television crews next came up just before our August vacation when we were due to stay in La Higuera for the first time. On one of my regular pestering calls the agent mentioned that the Zenith team was visiting to do some filming of progress on the property that was selected in place of ours. Keith and Vicki also mentioned that they were being interviewed for the series and that Vicki, who has a television background, had established a communication with Alan. So we thought that we might just meet up with the production team somewhere.

On the middle Sunday of our stay we met up with David and Edith near to Murcia to collect Mark who had been staying with them for a few days. He was to stop with us for a while and we were then to be joined by Kathy's parents a couple of days later. We had a quiet evening on the Sunday and on Monday were planning to head for the coast. But things turned out rather differently. Firstly, when I called the agent to pick his brains on telephone installations, he mentioned that he'd be out for most of the day because he was filming. You know the sort of thing, director's chair with your name on it, personal make up artist, best boy etc. That reminds me what is a "best boy"? Then he called back at 12:30, just as we heading off for our delayed drive, to ask us to meet up for lunch at the local municipal swimming pool, as the crew wanted to meet some people who had already been through the process. A sort of "one I prepared earlier" I suppose.

We had driven past the public pool but had been far too busy to try it out. That was a shame on two counts. Firstly it is large and nearly deserted, and secondly it is open only in July and August, meaning that the following day would be the last of the season. That meant that Mark had little opportunity to try it out - and so did we. We arrived at the pool as requested to find a bar and restaurant that we had not known about. We also met up with another couple who we spotted as fellow British and asked if they too were there to meet the production team. It turned out that it was their house that was being restored in front of the cameras and that they were taking a break from filming.

A few minutes later the Zenith team arrived, followed his customary fifteen minutes late by our agent. Kathy sat at one end of the table near the film crew and Mark and I sat at the other with him, with the Nichols in between. Mark and I had a very pleasant lunch, but we had no idea what was going on at the other end of the table. At one point and quite suddenly Alan Ravenscroft and co said their farewells and left, arranging to the Nichols shortly. I asked Kathy if she had enjoyed her lunch, which she had, and she said that she thought they wanted to come up to us at 4 o'clock. "What for?" I asked. "I think they want to film the house" came her reply. "You think?" "Well yes. They didn't seem very definite really."

The three of us had a quick swim and returned home to tidy up. The film team obviously knew nothing of Spanish habits, for here when you say 4pm you mean "not before 4 o'clock". But they were British and pulled up our drive at just 2 minutes to four. Soundman Mike, Director/cameraman Nick and their researcher scattered in various directions to establish what, if anything, was worthy of their production, while Alan chatted away and we compared notes about restoration processes in France and Spain. Shortly Nick called out to say that we would "do it up here".

A few minutes later and we were perched uncomfortably in our own patio chairs as they sunk under our weight into the dry soil of our neighbors' field looking down on our house below. It was hot and dry and we both felt especially fat that day. The interview was very pleasant and in it Alan covered the obvious questions, why here; what went wrong; how had we been accepted etc. We then sat through the whole thing again while Nick filmed Alan asking the questions from another angle, and included a few "noddies", where Alan nodded knowingly in our direction, as if in answer to our comments.

When the filming was over we were grateful to be allowed to put hats back on our heads and offered iced spring water or cups of tea all round. When you are really thirsty the local water is preferable to beer or tea and has the desired effect very speedily. It has the added advantage that it really is a very pleasant drink – not a chemical in sight. As we chatted once again to Alan the rest of them went off filming our house, inside, outside and from every angle available. Mike even took the camera at one point and lay on the floor to film our African sculpture, now complete with a stone plinth found by the side of the road.

Nick then persuaded Mark to water the geraniums while he filmed him and joked that he would now be immortalized as the "hose boy". He told him that he should be especially pleased as Mike had hoped to progress to be "hose boy". Perhaps it has something to do with being "Best boy"?

We asked what would happen next and were told that if they wanted to use us we would be sent the appropriate waiver of rights forms and they prepared to leave. Well we didn't receive those forms. But what did happen next was really quite fun. All through the filming Pepé and one of his team had been furiously digging out and boarding the area for the terrace, apparently in preparation for the concrete. What they did not explain was that the cement mixer was on its way as we finished filming. And just as Alan and co prepared to leave the cement mixer arrived.

The driver decided to reverse up our steep, narrow and windy drive. I still don't know why he thought that was a good idea. Next day his colleague arrived with load number two and drove straight up without a problem. He simply turned round at the back of our house. But the first driver had other ideas. It took over an hour to get the truck out of the hole he had made when he first became stuck. He decided that rather than drive out and try again he would keep revving the engine to get out of this little dip, which soon became so deep that the rear of the vehicle was resting on the right wheel and the centre of the axle.

At one point it started to tip very slightly and we all had visions of cement mixer on its side, spewing fast drying concrete in all directions and blocking our house with a rough-sided man made hill. Fortunately Pepé and his assistant came to the rescue and managed to shovel back more soil than the cement mixer spewed out. After a long and overheated interlude they eventually freed the truck to deliver his mix at around 6:30. At this point the film crew left and Mark decided to take us off to the coast for dinner.

The "House in Spain" series started around a month later and, although we obviously weren't going to be on it, Kathy methodically recorded every episode to show people what the area was like and so on. When the fifth episode was broadcast I was in Brussels attending a European board meeting. So it came as something of a surprise when Kathy called my mobile to say "We didn't look too fat or sound too stupid." It took me a few minutes to gather my thoughts as, at the time I was at dinner surrounded by fellow board members of eight nationalities. My boss Frank was seated opposite and told me to warn Kathy that he wanted to see a copy of the video – with her in a bikini.

Kathy's not much into bikinis, but Frank seemed impressed by the house none the less. It took ages for the release forms to arrive, but at least now if we do become famous it will be official.

11 - "The System"

Our little plot of land in Spain amounts to just a few acres. We have had gardens of various sizes in England, but never before have I considered myself a "land owner". Now I feel that I should be able to hold my own with the local farm owners in our village pub. Obviously their concerns may be on a somewhat grander scale than mine, and of course topics such as European Union grants and bovine TB are unlikely ever to benefit or to worry me. But I could imagine one day hanging up my briefcase and donning a cap and pipe as I claim my chair in the corner by the fire, where I would expound my theories on better land use and crop yields.

Of course I would not want to do anything too serious and I certainly would not want to get too involved in manipulating nature – it's really been too good to me to consider paying nature back in that way. My old chair is more likely now to be a bench outside the village bar, where the various small holders meet to share a *copa de tinto* (or several). They will spend many long hours comparing the state of the land, or the current rainfall. They will discuss the quantity and quality of the almond blossom as they estimate the size and hence the value of the crop.

The almond crop is important here, and so too are the olives. These smallholdings generate various proportions of wealth for the landowners around. For some it is no more than pin money, earned by weekend tilling in Spring and autumn and a couple of weeks almond picking in August or olive picking around January. Their neighbors by contrast may depend very heavily on the crops. Indeed for some it is still their only source of income. The value placed on these fields is not seen only in financial terms though, as there is an enormous respect for the land here, and for what it produces.

We discovered just how highly the crops are valued when we came to September that first year. All our attention had been directed at the house and the work being done there. We had arranged for someone to plough the weeds into our fields earlier in the year, but we had not taken the harvest very seriously. No, I shall re-phrase that, we ignored the harvest. Well we had a few other things on our minds. In August all our neighbors were out all day on Saturdays and Sundays in the hottest part of the day to ensure that the harvest was safely gathered in. By contrast I spent half an hour picking enough almonds from various trees to demonstrate the various types growing on our land, and to have the satisfaction of tasting our own almonds.

I was sure that we had been told that someone would look after these trees. We were told about "The System", whereby it is quite common for one smallholder to tend the trees of another in exchange for a large part of the crop, and that a similar deal existed for our produce. Someone (we knew not who) would plough the fields and tend the trees. They would pick the crop and would be allowed to sell the major part of what they picked. The balance would be delivered to us to sell eat or dispose of. Now bearing in mind my general lack of ability with things of a physical nature this seemed to me like a good deal.

But come September when all the fields around had been harvested our trees were still covered in nuts, which were drying out on the branches. I couldn't work out whether I had confused everyone by picking my meager carrier bag full in August, or whether some other error on my part left us with these almonds un-harvested. Our builder was always quick with explanations, and indeed one day his quick thinking may be his downfall, because I'm sure he doesn't always think things through. He explained that it is quite normal to leave a crop one year to enhance the crop the following year. And I'm still not sure to this day whether that is an informed judgement or a bit of thinking on the hoof. I would have thought that if that were the objective one would destroy the blossom or the young fruit to encourage the goodness to return to the tree rather than be wasted on fruit. The neighbors didn't seem at all convinced either, as they wanted to know why the fields had not been harvested. We invited them to help themselves, but this was not met with any action. I couldn't understand why because they all invite us to take fruit from their trees whenever we want.

It took me a while to learn the difference. The grapes, plums and oranges that Andréas gives us so generously are produce of the trees in his garden. The almonds on the other hand are from the trees in the fields and hence are commercial produce. He would probably regard neighbors who help themselves to his plums as friends enjoying the fruits of their friendship. By contrast it seems that if those same people picked a bag or two of nuts they would be seen as plunderers, raiding his hard earned stores. Thus no one would dream of "helping themselves" to our almonds. It would not be the done thing.

Our own land sits in various pockets to the west of the house and below. In fact the house sits on a sort of promontory to one side of the fields that make up our acres. When Andréas, as keeper of the boundaries, first took me to walk our land I was rather confused - and not for the last time, as you may gather. He explained that the three small fields immediately adjacent to the main drive are ours. That bit was easy. The next pocket of land he showed me was two fields across an access road. At some points only that access road separates them from the first three, but at others there are fields or odd shapes of terrain, which are not ours.

We also have three fields in the ravine behind us. But nothing connects these with the house or the rest of our land. In fact you would be hard pressed to argue any logical connection. The location of one of our fields requires that to enter it one must cross an unkempt triangle of scrubland. When I suggested to Andréas that I might cut back the weeds he pointed out to me that this was not our land. Not only does it serve as access to one of our fields, this field is quite inaccessible without crossing our land.

It seems that the process of inheritance is responsible. Under Spanish law property can go one of two ways on the death of the owner. If the deceased leaves behind very specific instructions regarding each of his assets then, subject to those instructions being lawful, his requests will be met. If however there is no will, or if that will is anything less than comprehensive, the state acts as executor. There are then two options, either the state takes the lot, or it just taxes the value and splits the assets amongst all the children and the spouse of the poor fellow who passed away.

The result is that various stretches of the countryside have been divided over the years into smaller and smaller pockets, which have become increasingly disconnected. Everyone then needs an Andréas to explain that this 100 square foot triangle of land belongs to Jorge's grandson, who lives on the other side of the valley and has never been near the place since old Jorge kicked the bucket.

It is because of this bizarre bit of latin law that our house is divided from some of its fields by an access road. Behind us the almond fields continue, but they are not ours. Patricio, whose brother sold us the house, has his property in front of ours. His land however is mainly behind us. To gain access he really needs to pass our house. Obviously this is no problem to us. After all he has been doing this since long before we arrived on the scene. And more to the point it provides an additional opportunity to keep contact with our neighbors and to be treated as part of the community.

Even so I was confused when one Sunday morning I was awoken at 7am by the unmistakable resonance of a small white van struggling up our drive. We certainly were not expecting Pepé that day, and by the sound of it this particular little white van had a rather poorly diesel engine. When it belched to a halt at the back of us I jumped up to forestall any possible entry by one of the builders. I was surprised to see a complete stranger unloading the large white sacks used for collecting almonds. He and his wife smiled and waved and disappeared over the brow of the hill, presumably to do their labors.

An hour or so later there had been no more sign of them, so we brewed four cups of strong coffee and took these and some pastries to make our introductions. I still haven't got a clue what their names are. This is not because they haven't told me. It is simply because I could not understand a word they said. I did manage to grasp the idea that they lived around two miles away across the valley and that this single small field was theirs. We all sat under one of their trees shaded by our straw hats and chatted together for half an hour or so. It was most enlightening, in a sort of "how did we manage to fill so much time and understand so little?" sort of a way.

We didn't see them again after that day. We have never bumped into them in the market or any of the shops, someone else arrived next spring to plough the field, and we wait to see if they turn up again one Sunday in August to harvest it. When I asked one of our neighbors who they are I got a very strange look. Do you remember the sort of expression that grandmothers apparently used to wear to accompany the "We don't talk about what happened to Auntie Sible in this house thank you" type of comment? Well this was the expression we were given, and not a jot of information was conveyed with it.

The best of our almond trees bears superb nuts, sweet and almost milky in texture. Patricio explained that when he and his brothers were boys they would watch this particular tree willing the nuts to ripen. It was never the first to be ready for harvest, but fortunately it was not the last either. By the time these fields are harvested the husks on this tree's fruit have split and peeled back, making the fruit all the easier to remove. It seems that once harvest began all those years ago the young boys would make a labor of love out of cropping this particular tree, because they were allowed to consume a small proportion of what they picked.

It hadn't occurred to me that we might have different varieties of almonds on our smallholding. I don't know why I had not thought of it; after all it is perfectly normal to find several varieties of apple in a traditional orchard. Growers of old would not have been concerned with mass-market standardization and would probably have taken what was available. If they did think about it they might rather have considered that a mix of varieties might be a better hedge against failure or disease. I first wondered what might be the difference in our first blossoming. In late February when the almond trees produce that delicate pinkish white blossom I saw that some of our trees were pinker than others. And was concerned that some had already lost their blossom before others had burst their buds.

It was much later in summer as the fruit formed and filled that I saw just how different our various trees were. I should have appreciated the differing stature of the various trees, but with the fruit in view it was impossible to miss the distinctive differences. Some were small almost round and very tightly packed, while at the other end of the spectrum those on Patricio's favorite tree were long full and a much deeper brown in color. As we waited for the trees to be harvested that first year, and as nothing happen I watched Patricio look at that tree whenever he came to see us. During one trip I decided that if the harvest had not been safely gathered in by the time I returned I would invite Patricio to join me and a bottle of *Jumilla* so that he could show me just how I should harvest my almonds. And I decided that his favorite was the tree on which I would ask him to teach me.

Having arrived back very late one evening I rose bright the next day and told Kathy that I had decided that "Patricio's tree" should be harvested as not to do so would be an appalling waste. I said no more and left her confused and half-asleep. I dashed down the lane and turned in Patricio's house, which was strangely quiet. I knew that he was not a late riser, so I had no compunction in knocking on the door. But reply came there none. I assumed that they had set off early to shop or to visit friends. When I returned to Kathy though I found out that they had returned to Barcelona a few weeks early because they were missing their little granddaughter. As a result he went away thinking that this unfeeling foreigner would waste the fruit of the land on which his family had labored so hard and for so many years.

Later that morning two little white vans pulled up on the road. I didn't recognize the occupants, but by the time we returned from town a few hours later the vans were gone – and so were all our almonds, including those from Patricio's tree. Around twenty pounds of various almonds had been left on our doorstep, obviously our share. It seemed that "The System" did work after all. But none of the nuts left for us were the ones from Patricio's tree.

12 - Hooray for Hollywood

We've all heard of "Spaghetti Westerns" – made cheaply in Italy by the mini moguls of Hollywood looking for cheap locations and even cheaper "extras", to enable them to create B movies on low budgets. Cowboys and Indians type films were big box office business in the sixties before the enormous success of Star Wars led to a whole new class of films where the cowboys were replaced by the adventurers of space and the Indians by the threatening forces of another galactic culture. The move into science fiction has meant that we have now stopped depicting these particular fellow humans as some sort of second-rate race, and it seems that political correctness has taken the place of conflict.

In some parts of North America I know that the Native Americans and the inheritors of the settlers are living in a degree of harmony. In others though it looks from my perspective as if persecution persists, and of course land disputes are an ongoing source of anguish to the natives. The same thing is true in so many captured lands. The aborigines describe horrific treatment. Man can be very cruel to his fellows, and we have an almost unique ability in nature to treat others of our own race as prisoners or exiles in their own lands.

It is also interesting to note that the more peaceful, gentle and unthreatening the original inhabitants may be the more aggressive and destructive the invading force. It is a lesson in human conflict to note what happened in Australia, by contrast with the situation in New Zealand. The Australian aborigines were overrun by the European invasion and totally overpowered. They lost land, children, wealth, dignity and self-respect. To this day the native Australians suffer enormous hardship and anxiety at the hands of the incoming society. By contrast the proud warrior race of the New Zealand Maoris fought hard and established early on that they would take no truck from these foreign arrivals. They have still had to face change imposed upon them, but have had far more influence on the implementation of that change and have lost less of their heritage or self respect. It

is an indictment that man must fight to keep what is rightfully his in what is meant to be an age of sophistication.
The move away from depicting the natives of any country as second class to their invaders is to be welcomed, even if we continue to see the same basic images in the imaginary lands of science fiction. The death of the western genre of movies has led to a change in the requirements of the film industry, and today directors look more for the dunes of North Africa, representative of space topography, than for the arid mountain scenes of New Mexico or Arizona. Thus Spaghetti Westerns died a death, and with them their lesser known Spanish equivalent, the "Paella Western".
My colleague Javier, a director in our Spanish partner organization, tells me that his father helped to put Almería on the map. Or perhaps I should say that he helped to put it on the big screen. He introduced the filmmakers to the splendors of the Sierras and created a bit of New Mexico near the sea. So it was that a few years ago a few cinema hits, many cheap movies and a number of low audience television programs were being made in the hills between Almería and Sorbas. Just a few blockbusters were part of the list, apparently including "A Fistful of Dollars" and "Indiana Jones".
It was big business. The sons of the land and the sea found themselves playing gold rush opportunists in the background, while minor stars and even a few well-known names were playing the important parts in front of them. The brothels and bars were depicted by tatty film set style facades, and the locals looked on in amazement at the lifestyle of these foreign style filmmakers. I say foreign style because many of these films were made without an American ever crossing the border of the set – in some cases they didn't even enter the country. And many of the movies made here were Spanish language films aimed at a non-American market.
In February we had a day to fill. Apollonia's hostal is not designed to spend all day. We could not get together with the builders and we had little need to wander around the local shops again. So we saddled up and headed off into the hills. Well actually we loaded ourselves into our little hire car and drove on one of our exploratory ventures, with the objective of getting to know the area. We were in Ollula del Rio on the road to Baza when I saw the sign to Macael and suggested to Kathy that we head over the mountains. The Sierra de los Filabres are impressive at any time of year, but in winter they are outstanding. We drove in brilliant sunshine from the warm dry

valley up to the snow line, and watched the almost alpine scenery to our left and the dry, brown valley below.
Having reached the highest point we had the obvious options of turning back or carrying on. We chose the latter – it must be the adventurer in our souls! At this point we were over 6500 feet above sea level and three times as high as our new property, and from here we could see so far that it was impossible to judge the distance accurately. We were close to the *Calar Altar* the highest point in the *Filabres*. We were around 25 miles from the east coast and 15 from the south, but the sea was clearly visible to us between the hills. And heading for the southern coast would bring us to Almería city. Or at least it would have done if we had made it that far.
We headed down towards Almería and reached the N340, the old road from Almería to the eastern seaboard of the province. We drove past the most amazing, almost out of this world sight of a massive solar energy park. The resourceful peoples of Spain have established that the heat and energy of the sun might as well be tapped for uses other than ripening fruit and ripening the tans of countless Scandinavian bodies. This solar plant comprises of row upon row of mirrors, reflecting the light of the sun as a concentrated beam in one bright central spot. This was the highlight of my day and we still take visitors to wonder at the scale and technology. One of the most startling aspects is the reflected light which is shed by the solar panels, and the idea that these few acres of panels can usefully trap enough energy to be worthwhile makes me appreciate how much of the Sun's energy must be wasted.
We stopped at a roadside bar, located opposite the gates. Even though it was the middle of winter we were becoming dehydrated and knowing the value of drinking plenty of water stopped for a few glasses. While there we shared a few small plates of tapas and marveled at the view across the road. No roadside diner can have such an amazing aspect. After an open-mouthed half-hour and a few more snaps in the camera we carried on. The road junction is at the small town of Tabernas, around a mile from the theme park. Tabernas is built around a pointed hill, which has a small Moorish castle at its pinnacle. There isn't much to be said in favor of Tabernas, which, though not unpleasant, is just another small town. But the castle is something else. Here Ferdinand and Isobel were holed up during the siege of Almería. The shame is that there is no information to be had, so to visit this attraction one needs to be a little more adventurous than most tourists. The views are exceptional, and

we were safe from any risk of tourist buses dumping their loads of passengers. In fact, once again, we were alone.
We turned right towards the city and saw the signs for Mini Hollywood. We knew it was there of course, but hadn't actually planned to visit. We've been with the boys to Universal Studios in California and to Disney MGM Studios in Orlando, so we reckoned we knew a thing or two about film set tours. And one thing we had learned is that you don't arrive late in the morning if you want to avoid the crowds. We once spent over two hours travelling, or rather not travelling, through horrendous Los Angeles traffic to get from our hotel to the Universal site. The result was that by the time we arrived the car parks were bursting and every attraction had queues an hour long. Mark and Paul had been very patient in the car, but exhaustion and frustration marred the day. We did not want to make the same mistake at Mini Hollywood, and would obviously normally have planned a visit to avoid the crush.
We need not have worried! When we drove past there were none of the expected queues so we acted on impulse - us? We followed the signs and remembered what we had read in the literature produced to promote the place. The leaflets and adverts talked about a feeling of being back in the old west. They explained that we could put ourselves in the place of the great movie directors, and led us to expect stunt shows and the like. We knew of course that we would have a choice of eateries - a flavor of the west perhaps. So we anticipated a little bit of sophistication in the desert of southern Almería.
As we headed towards Almería from Tabernas we saw the signs more often, but still saw no sign of crowds. It was February after all, and I imagine that even Universal Studios or Disney have quiet days. We would be able to enjoy the fun of the film set without all the crowds. And we did. There was not a crowd to be seen. We came upon the souvenir shop and publicity office and stopped to ask a few questions, but the office was closed. We looked across the ravine to where the stockade and a number of the sets could be seen.
The notice told us to continue for a few hundred yards to find the main entrance. We did as directed and turned off the main road onto the access road. As you will have gathered by now there was no throng of car park attendants or security staff, and we drove alone towards the entrance. I assumed that this particular tourist attraction must be as firmly shut as the information office that we had just left. But I was wrong. There at a Wild West style entrance was a ticket agent taking the money and

monitoring entry. We paid our money – around 1,500 pesetas ($10) each from memory, and joined the three other cars in the car park. I'm not sure, but at least two of those may have belonged to staff.

I'm not sure how busy Mini Hollywood gets these days, even in the height of the tourist season, but I don't think it can be too frenetic, as the total parking area available would suggest that not too many cars or coaches ever park there. There simply isn't that much parking space. We met one other group of visitors, a rather excitable little boy and his parents. He was anxious to see the stunt shows and had to be satisfied with the rather smelly collection of bison, camels and goats. Goats?? You don't see too many of them when John Wayne struts his stuff now do you.

The car park is directly outside the main square of the fake cowboy community that has been constructed here, so we didn't have to look for car park shuttle buses or moving walkways to find our way in. And to be honest it was all rather sad. We made our way into the bar and hotel. The leaflets had promised catering facilities, and this seemed to be all of them. Inside were a couple of rather sad looking characters, dressed in Stetson and chaps. They had obviously been playing their parts for some time, and looked at us as if to say that their job would be more fun without us.

They had little choice to offer – indeed beer, Coke and packets of potato chips are my memory of the list, but I think there was more. We chose Coke and a packet of crisps each, and as we sat down at a rather authentic looking table – well it was pretty shot up – we were surrounded by cats of every shape and size. They obviously had a penchant for crisps, and hence most of our snack went down their throats rather than ours. I suppose we should thank them for aiding us in our rather forlorn attempts to shed some weight. There must have been 15 of them, all offspring of the same father from several different litters.

We had a wander around looking at the film promotion photos of stars I did not know. Many of them had Hispanic sounding names, and a number of the movies sounded equally un-American. Every so often a big name cropped up, and even one or two film names I recognized, but there was nothing on these photos to say that they were actually filmed here.

Outside the bar we spent the few minutes it took to walk around the film lot. I was really impressed – yes really – by the number of different locations possible in such a small space. We walked from a gold rush town into a hick cowboy site, an Indian encampment and a Mexican hacienda. Round every corner we found ourselves in a different set. The back of an American bank would be a Mexican jail. The planning that created this is very clever and I take off my hat to the set designers and builders of the past who created this facility – well I would if I were wearing one right now.

I was disappointed. There can be no hiding the fact. The hype promised so much more. We were later to read in a tourist guide that there is a smaller, competing, cowboy film park less than a mile away, which trades on the success of its larger name sake, but it apparently has few of the facilities of the real Mini Hollywood. Were we at the replica, in which case where is the larger, genuine article to be found? Or is there a smaller less well-endowed competitor nearby.

We shall return to see Mini Hollywood in season - one day - and we shall find the answers to those questions. But for now I'm just grateful that Mini Hollywood has almost none of the glitz, crush and commercialism of its namesake. It is nice to be able to experience the thrill of California once in a lifetime – but I am very fortunate that I do not have to live in it. Hooray!

13 - Late Night Deliveries

I'm not much of a late night person. I can often be found in wintertime comfortably curled up with a book in front of the log fire, or watching TV. In my life I have served on many committees, and, as the other members of those that I have chaired would testify, I am pretty good at bringing things to a conclusion soon after 9pm. This is not only to concentrate the mind. That said though I do abhor meetings that ramble – I judge that my time is worth more than to go over and over the same topic several times only to confirm an agreement reached an hour previously.

I have a reputation for impatience in meetings, and I suppose, if I am honest, that the reputation is justified. I can be ungenerous to my fellow committee members who may not have grasped the blindingly obvious quite as rapidly as I. And I often find myself apologizing for snapping at someone along the lines of "Of course this is the right solution – it's patently clear".

The other reason for bringing meetings to a sensible conclusion at that time of night is that much later and I'm use to neither man nor beast. I have traveled extensively in my life, both for pleasure and on business. And I find travel on business an increasingly tedious way to spend my time. This is especially true as, like most conscientious businessmen, I do most of my travelling in my time, rather than in conventional office hours. Thus it is that at 7pm, when many of the staff have left to go home, I pack up my papers in my Brussels office to do the same thing. The difference of course is that my home is a flight and a car journey away. At the other end of the day I regularly leave home in the dark to enable me to get to one meeting or another in time for a 9:30 start.

This all makes my evenings even more precious and hence I am always surprised to meet other people who do not view an evening at home with the same imperative.

In Spain of course things don't start to liven up much before 9pm. Well that is to say that where things liven up at all they don't tend to do so any earlier. Certainly in the big towns and resorts the Spanish don't expect to eat or to be entertained any earlier than that, and it is quite normal for restaurants to start filling up at 10:30pm. Even in our backwoods part of rural Spain hotel restaurants will open at 9pm, and for stand-alone bars and restaurants to sit empty until late in the evening is not unusual.

What we regard as traditionally daytime activities tend to run well into the night. Pedro's work on hanging our doors, which started at 9pm, is testimony to the fact

Actually several things seem to have happened at that time of night – including the arrival of the local gas company representative. He had to come to check the quality of the gas installation to ensure our safety, and to complete the contract for our supply. It was dusk as he and his colleague arrived, and it was pitch black by the time they left. They did a through job though, and we both felt reassured that our gas equipment would not let us down, blow up or poison us in operation.

Those two marble pillars, which we bought on impulse as the base for our new dining table, were delivered at 9:30pm. That August evening was hot and decidedly stormy. At about 8 o'clock the clear blue skies of the day started to cloud over and they were storm clouds that took the place of the blue.

Half an hour later the heavens opened and for 90 minutes it bucketed down. The glazier came and went as the rains were building up, and the freshly cut top for this new feature was carefully carried in by four of us across the wet muddy forecourt and into the dining hall. By the time that our *marmoles* man had arrived I had decided that getting his van close to the front door was a priority. Because the house has three external doors, and because we have all-round access for vehicles, we were able this wet and stormy night to get deliveries through the nearest door. This way we could ensure that the delivery van could be parked as close as possible to the final resting place of the new pillars.

When the conversion work was in hand Pepé removed an old worn marble step to replace it with a brand new one, just like the steps, which he had installed at the back doors. We decided that we did not want to loose this original feature and so later on in the process we had Pepé re-install our original marble pillar at the front door. Patricio, whose family home this once was, was delighted that we had seen fit to keep this stone on which his father had sharpened knives, and he had played ball many years ago. He became quite tearful as he talked about it, and told us several times how much it meant to him that we had bothered to recover the step.

Under Latin Skies

At the time we asked for its re-instatement neither of us quite realised that in putting it back we were creating an obstacle for our visitors and ourselves. The new steps at the back are gentle and easily negotiated. The old one, once back in its rightful place, is high and narrow, so we know that we will have to build another step below it to ease our way in. And as we become frailer little features that ease our mobility will become increasingly important.

To return to the pillars torrents of rain and the shiny step made treacherous territory for us to cross at the best of time, but when our marble delivery driver arrived alone I realised that we had another handicap – me! I am strong enough, but I can be a bit cack-handed. When the driver called me to help I dashed to the rescue and was drenched in seconds.

We lifted the first of the two pillars off the side of the truck and struggled towards the front door. For some reason I found myself in my usual position – walking backwards in the direction of a hazard. I'd have made good material for the Key Stone Cops or Ealing Comedies. I might even have fed the processes of the famous Whitehall Farces. I'm sure the directors of those old grainy black and white "chase" movies must have relished watching people like me – and no doubt they would have kept a good distance between us.

As we carried our burden across the front drive I forgot that there is a raised pavement running the length of the front of the house. I was reminded speedily enough though as my heel struck the step. We were wet, in the dark and carrying half a ton of marble – and I stumbled. I can only judge from his later reactions, but I reckon that I put the fear of all that's holy into my newfound Spanish co-worker. I did recover though – I'm usually quite good at recovering. Having crossed the pavement we then had to negotiate the raised step --our preserved marble, and as I lifted one enormous marble construction I lifted my now sore foot to step up onto another.

We did it. The first pillar arrived safely and unscathed into its new home in our dining room. I cannot say that the two of us suffered as little as the plinth. At this point I was wet and a little sore, but I was feeling quite pleased with myself. Manuel – we were on first name terms by now – reminded me that the job was only half done, as we still had another one to bring inside. I suggested a beer, or a coffee, or frankly anything, to delay the second weight lifting session.

It was then that Manuel reminded me that he had already been driving for half an hour in various attempts to find our house, which at this point did not yet benefit from the very individually presented name sign fitted by own fair hands. He was wet and tired and wanted to go home while he still had the energy to do so. So without a break we stumbled back to the van and lifted the now very wet and very slippery second pillar. We made it. I didn't stumble once second time around and we placed this heavy object just where it needed to be.

At this point Manuel left, delighted no doubt to have escaped unscathed. But Kathy and I realized that the glass top would probably weigh as much as either of the pillars. It is over half an inch thick and seven feet by three foot six in surface. At this point it was propped against the wall near to the table, so distance was not a problem. Our problem would obviously be the weight and the odd shape. We looked at it. We touched it. We made our first move to lift it, and then we appreciated the obvious solution to our problem. We left it exactly where it was and next day asked the workmen to help me lift it in place. Once put in its correct place it looked superb and will for years to come.

I am used to the sort of deliveryman who says he'll be there three weeks on Thursday, but refuses to give any more clue, such as time of day. That's how things work in the UK, but not here. As you see our marble and our glass were prepared and delivered later on the day we ordered them. And the really surprising thing is that neither Manuel the *marmoles* man, nor *Christaleria Garcia* demanded payment in advance. I tried to pay the glazier a deposit, but he looked rather nervous and told me that it was impossible. Not unnecessary you note, but impossible. He doesn't work like that and it seems that no one else does either.

We purchased various bits of furniture from various shops in the area. The choice in the cities is certainly better, but we like to support local business when we can. We also assumed at first that being 40 minutes away from the "big" stores would be some sort of handicap, especially as La Higuera is in the middle of no-where. But we were wrong. Having taken delivery of the various parts of our new dining table we went in search of dining chairs to go with it. Well we both went and Kathy searched. We looked at cane chairs, and wrought iron chairs. We tried pine chairs and antique looking chairs. But eureka style Kathy shouted in Mer el Muebles that she had found exactly what she wanted. Note that please – exactly what <u>she</u> wanted.

There were six nicely crafted chairs in a mid-brown wood, with comfy padded seats covered in a bright Mediterranean yellow.

They would go perfectly in our white walled house, and sit well on the terracotta floor. The problem was that there were six chairs and we wanted eight. Now we all know what that means – a special order, a six-week wait and two chairs that don't quite match the original six. But even knowing all that Kathy set her heart on them – she's good at doing that. So we asked the manager if it would be possible to have 8 of this particular chair. He told us that he didn't have them in stock, but he didn't once suck sharply between his teeth as British workmen are trained to do.

He didn't even ask for a deposit – we should not have been surprised. He took our address and mobile phone number and promised to see what he could do. This was 1:45, and the shop was about to shut for the traditional three hour lunch break, so we went off down to the front in Garrucha and had a beer while we decided what needed to be done next. It was Friday afternoon and that evening we had invited Keith and Vicki plus some friends of theirs to supper. It was the middle of August and so we had no plans to eat inside. The garden furniture was ideal for this occasion. We had to do some shopping, but otherwise decided that the afternoon was our own to relax.

Half way through that beer the phone rang. It was Mer el Muebles to say that they had managed to locate 8 of the chairs we had chosen. Good news. "Would it be ok to deliver them that evening?" was the question. That evening; no six-week wait; no extended negotiations to get them delivered. We gave him our address and our now well-rehearsed directions and settled back to the beer, wondering if the driver would find our un-named house.

Our guests arrived to eat at around 8:30 and we settled down to a few glasses of *cava,* Spain's superb champagne style sparkling wine, as we enjoyed the cool of evening and shared the views. It was about 9:15 that we decided to serve some food, and just then, as if it had been planned, we saw the furniture shop's lorry driving up the neighboring drive. I called out to him to take the *entrada proxima* and within a few moments a great big furniture lorry was backing up our drive to the front door. The sky was clear and the sun was setting, but these were professionals. They drove perfectly and on arrival they admired our glass table with more than adequate enthusiasm.

They then carefully unloaded each chair and placed them all exactly around the table. This new furniture sits within a border of patterned tiles set in the floor designed for the purpose long before we knew just what sort of table we would buy. And the lorry driver and his mate lovingly arranged the chairs exactly to ensure symmetry. Not one of them was out of place and they provided the perfect complement to the table. Hello magazine would have been proud of us. Well they might if they had ever heard of us.

Like the other deliverymen they did their job speedily and efficiently and went on their way. This left us to enjoy our meal by candlelight, and we brought to the table a tray of cold cut meats and cheeses, salads, bread and good wine. It was 10pm and we all shared and enjoyed this late night delivery.

14 - Las Cuevas

When Edith my mother in law brought over the details of houses in rural Almería I was particularly struck by the property on the front page of the estate agent's blurb. *Cortijo las Cuevas* is a long two-story building, which "could be occupied almost immediately". It didn't say whether you would have to be a goat to want to, but the picture and the description intrigued me. It apparently had 5 rooms downstairs and one large room above. Three of the downstairs rooms were caves, which explained why the lower storey was so much larger than the upper, despite the building looking very evenly spread between the two. This house had been build in front of a cliff face and three caves had been carved out behind the ground floor of the building.

The upper floor was just a room running the length of the house. Many of these older properties have a first floor, but like *Cortijo Oliverico*, our first choice, the upper floor was used for grain and feed store. Often that floor would be constructed to support a few sacks and maybe a goat or two. They were not build with furniture and people in mind, and most certainly were not designed to be lived in. So this charming farmhouse was really a single story dwelling house with storage above.

But the potential was enormous. I knew this without even visiting it. Part of the potential lay in the price – just 2.5 million pesetas, or $16,000 in real money. Yes $16,000 for a solidly built character home with potential. You wouldn't get a parking space for that price in Brussels. In fact you wouldn't get many new cars for that price. But of course the words "character" and "potential" can hide a host of hidden dangers, and who was to say that this was any different. The real appeal of this photo was the fact that the house had caves. It had never occurred to me before that you might have a house with living space in hillside caves. I knew of course that troglodyte living was a part of our history, and I had even heard of hill-face houses with a cave or two used as storage or stabling. I knew that the French word *cave* was used to describe a cellar, whether built or hued from the earth, and by implication that a *cueva* in Spanish might be a cellar or a cave. But I hadn't clicked that *cueva* might also be a room in a domestic dwelling, which had been excavated from the rock.

I wanted *Cortijo las Cuevas*. It sounded idyllic, set on a hillside with outstanding views, or some such realtor's blurb. And of course it was only 2.5 million pesetas. It was obviously meant to be ours. I phoned immediately to say we'd pop over in a few weeks and to request the agent to "reserve" it for us. How foolish. The man who answered told me that the property list I had in front of me was over a month out of date and that this particular house had been sold before the list even hit the street. He also, very patiently, explained that they operated on a first come first served basis. He had no intention of reserving anything on the basis of an international phone call at 9 o'clock at night from a complete stranger. On reflection I decided that this man was no fool. I would take the same approach in his position. And as we discovered when we lost *Cortijo Oliverico* you ain't got it till you've done the formalities.

The hills around Granada and Almería are rich in cave dwellings. Indeed parts of Andalucía are dotted with settlements carved into the hills. Many of them were inhabited and abandoned hundreds of years ago. The invading Moors chased local people off their own lands and cave farmers were amongst those who left. So as you drive around in the hills of the *Sierras* you will often catch sight of cave entrances. They rarely if ever sit alone. The troglodytes were obviously a gregarious people, as the caves tend to be carved in communities. Presumably if a cliff is a good place to cut one cave it must be just as suitable for others. Several of the dwellings are individual, and there are signs that others are connected. A pathway between three or four caves may well mean that these were really different rooms of the same home. Some would have housed the family, while others would accommodate the livestock or the feed. Some dwellers were less particular allowing the animals, the children and the grain to live side by side in one cave.

Then there are the current settlements, where modern day troglodytes live in a home created by carving out of the rock, but with all the trappings of modern day life. These homes are comfortable, and sometimes quite luxurious. Today they adopt many of the characteristics of modern design, with stone paint effects on the outside "walls", smart front doors and even double-glazed windows! Inside they would be hard to distinguish from any other home. The walls may not be as square as those in a modern house, and there may not be as many windows, but the attention to detail can be just as striking. These homes can be large, even spacious, and can demonstrate the owner's personality just as easily as any other home.

Some have gardens, or garages, cut from the rock just like the home alongside. Others have a second story, usually accessed by outside steps, but at least one we've seen has an internal staircase and four separate bedrooms, as well as the usual kitchen, bathroom and living space. The plumbing works just as it should and the waste is carried away to a cesspit, just as in most other rural properties around. Most of these homes sport television aerials, and some even have satellite dishes stuck on the rock-face nearby. These TV viewers have the advantage that they can plonk their receivers high up to get better reception. The downside is that if your particular rock faces the wrong way you may not get any reception at all.

These homes run much lower fuel bills than most. In summer they benefit from the constant internal temperature, which provides a pleasantly cool environment in which to escape the heat of the sun. In winter, by contrast, that same constant temperature means that the chill of a winter evening can easily be shut out and far less heating is needed to ensure comfort. Heating is often provided by an electric fire or a gas stove. But more often a wood burning stove or an open fire is built in to the home. As a result it is not uncommon to see chimneys rising out of the cliffs, and sometimes the chimney may be on one face, while the entrance to the home is on another. Inside they can be quite a labyrinth of rooms. It is not uncommon for one window and door to lead through the main living room into several bedrooms, storerooms and the like.

The modern cave inhabitant is a fully integrated member of modern Andalucían society. They drive cars and shop in the same supermarkets as the rest of us, and they entertain themselves in the same way as their local neighbors. But they have something extra about them. They have independence and self-esteem that so many lack today. These are features of rural life generally, but at this extreme end of rural living they are more acute. These folk have often inherited their homes, although ownership is rarely recorded formally in any state register. Others have chosen to adopt this life style, either because they seek the simple life, or because of the low cost.

One university behavioral scientist undertook a major study of life in cave dwellings a few years ago. He looked at the life style, the quality of life, sanitation, eating habits, working lives and relationships. He studied education and identified current parental attitudes to the preparation of their offspring for life, and he looked at the inter-relationships between these people and their cave dwelling neighbors, and between them and the rest of society. He was surprised to uncover – nothing. These folk are just like the rest of us. Now that really is a revelation. They have similar values, although they tend to apply them more consistently. They have similar work patterns to their rural neighbors, and they enjoy good relationships with their house dwelling neighbors. The people who have the hang-ups he discovered are those amongst us who live in towns and assume that anyone who lives in a cave must beat up his wife with a club and go hunting wild animals to feed his poor and disease ridden family. It's not like that. One of the men he met had lived in a cave since he was married, and now in his fifties couldn't think why everyone didn't do the same. When our esteemed professor asked him whether he would like to live in an apartment near to his work, with nice clean facilities etc. he received the reply "But I couldn't live in an apartment block. My donkey would not be happy going up and down in an elevator". Now that's home spun philosophy for you.

The north south motorway is around half an hour away from our village house. It runs from the French border in the north to Almería in the south. Work is underway to connect this with the Malaga section, which will mean that it continues as far as Algeciras, the southern tip of the Iberian Peninsular. In fact if you were to carry on across the border with France you could travel by motorway all the way round to the toe of Italy, or in almost any other direction across Europe's network of motorways. The section near to us is known as "*autovia*" rather than "*autopista*". This describes a sort of minor highway, with the benefit that it is always toll free. These free and usually empty motorways make the task of getting around all the more pleasant.

Just south of our junction with the motorway is the town of *Cuevas del Almanzora*. This town is named after ancient cave settlements that line the hills in this part of the valley. Today the town is a thriving, even bustling, community, with light industry and agricultural support businesses. It has a population of around 9,000, and is a part of the district of Vera. The caves are all around, but the main community is clearly sign posted to one side of the town. A year or so earlier Edith and David had spent a few days with friends in the nearby resort of Mojacar. They had driven over the hills and found a cave settlement not far away, where the inhabitants had proudly shown off their homes and

welcomed these visitors like long-lost friends. At Easter we decided to go in search of caves and started our hunt in *Cuevas del Almanzora*. This was not the place where they had been so well received, but it gave us the chance to show Paul and Mark that this life style really did exist.
We followed the signs. I was in the lead in a Ford Galaxy, and was followed by Edith and David's Fiat Punto. The route took us along the *rambla* and up the side of the hills. Here we found a settlement of around 25 homes. Each was individually decorated and apart from the odd and uneven facades they could easily have been in any other lovingly cared for street. The hard-core roadway took us along the little front gardens and past the front doors and windows, until we found ourselves in what seemed to be a farmyard. At this point we had a problem. I could not back up, partly because the other car was behind us, but largely because this big van I was driving was as wide as the road in parts. So I carried on, with no idea of what I might encounter. A few goats and a clutch of chickens later we moved from one farmyard into another, and then into another, which led us into someone's garden. By this time I was too committed to go back and smiled sweetly at the confused widow, dressed in black, who was hanging her rather personal washing to dry.
Washing is usually a private matter in Spain, and it certainly is not done to hang it out in public. So I imagine that to invade someone's hanging area is a fairly major social crime. I did the only thing I could do and carried on with the family embarrassed and confused, but still in tow. Fortunately we were on the verge of escape as this garden led onto an unmade track that took us away from all this. I managed to extricate the borrowed car I was driving unscathed and got out of there pretty sharpish. The shame is that we didn't get a very close look at the caves we passed, as everyone was more concerned about my ability to get us out with minimum embarrassment.
I've continued playing around with plans for our house here and, once we can afford it we plan to add some more rooms and a swimming pool at the back as part of an Andalucían style courtyard. We also hope to replace that walled patio at the front with the new master bedroom suite, and to provide a more permanent home for the name of our house. As part of that project we want to build a roof terrace on top – and I want a cellar constructed below to provide storage space and an ideal climate to keep and mature wine. How long I can keep it for has yet to be proven, but in years to come I will potter happily around in my underground workshop. My own little *cueva*.

Under Latin Skies

15 - The Locals

A great deal happened on our fist day visiting this haven in the south of Spain. Among other places the realtor took us to see a little town house in the village where we have now settled. This village seems to generate a degree of unrest as those of our neighbors who live at the northern end of the village know that where they reside is the real village. After all they have the Church, the bakers, the village shop and 2 bars. Down at our end we have none of these advantages.

We just have each other - and a village sign. For right opposite our house is the only boundary sign that this village has. It proves that ours is the most southerly property, and there can be no doubt as to the official position. But to the locals who have argued for years the council's view of things is really rather an irrelevance. After all they have their well-honed prejudices to prove their case. Why on earth would they be interested in the facts? One fact that does confuse things occasionally is the exact wording of the sign. Over the months we have seen various letters disappear and re-appear to create some interesting, and sometimes not very coherent alternatives. We reckon one of those nere-do-wells from the other end of the village is responsible, but I wouldn't dream of ever saying so. The village is around two miles from north to south and, apart from the Church square area, it is rather spread out.

The house that we first visited in the little *plaza,* not as the name might suggest at the Church end of things. In fact it is a rather nice little square, recently refurbished with marble-edged flowerbeds, off the main road and a few hundred yards from us. The agent showed us a small but well maintained terrace house. A single story house it had been built in the gaps between three others. It had a pleasant enough courtyard at the back, but we had a dream of one day having our own swimming pool (indeed we still dream about it) and this place was not designed with swimming pools in mind. There was actually quite a bit of land with this house, but it was in two parcels on the other side of the open square. That is apart from the square itself of which we would have been the proud owners of one fifth. It seems that each of the properties bordering this little square owns and tends a piece of the terrain. The bit belonging to this house had obviously been well maintained, but I'm not much of a gardener at the best of times, and I was quite sure I'd let the neighbors down.

The rest of the land was amongst other fields down by the *rambla*. It was good quality market gardening land and a couple of almond fields, but there was no logical way of establishing a private or even semi-private swimming pool area. I suppose that we could have trotted across the road in our kegs – but I don't really see it. Added to which we're not really the type to sit outside our front door as a way of relaxation. When Kathy's parents first moved to Spain they were in a fairly built up area, and their Spanish neighbors would sit outside on the terrace in the evening watching the television, which was strategically positioned inside the house in direct line of vision through the front door.

This seems to be quite common practice over here, especially in urban areas, and stems I presume from the fact that houses heat up during the day and in the evenings it can often be cooler outside than in. We have often seen families grouped outside their homes peering in through the windows or the door, and I imagine that the television has simply got in the way of an age-old habit of outdoor living. Some have taken the next obvious step and brought the TV set outside with them, and it is not uncommon to find two or three sets outside adjoining houses tuned to two or three different channels. Of course the family all talk while they're watching their favorite soap opera or game show, and, like Apollonia they shout at the presenters and the participants. All at the same time, and all at the tops of their voices. The volume then gets turned up to overcome the neighborly interference and the cacophony reaches epic proportions that would wake the dead.

That was in the suburbs of Barcelona, but the general principle might still apply, and I for one was having no part of it. We had just made our minds up that, nice though it was, this house was not meant for us, when the neighbors came along to introduce themselves. Two black-dressed roundly proportioned elderly ladies arrived from across the square and talked 20 to the dozen. They obviously knew the sales agent, and hence knew why he had brought us there. We talked about the outstanding potential of the house, and the pleasant situation.

We had been talking about replacing the rather worn wooden doors; shutters and windows with carefully matched modern replacements, and were looking at the damage to the front door. One of our new friends noticed this and took my arm. She led me round the corner with Kathy in tow. The objective was to show us her own house, of which she was justly proud. It seems that her late husband had done most of the work himself, and clearly she had looked after it well since his death. He had handcrafted the bedroom furniture and kitchen cabinets, and the decorating made it look like a 1970s revival. In London they'd pay the a television DIY team a fortune to re-create what we saw.
Her son had moved out once he married and had since moved on to Barcelona. (There you are the Barcelona connection again!) And it seemed that his room had been preserved as a sort of shrine to his youth – just the way that mothers keep their children's rooms throughout the "civilized" world. But she did not take us to see any of these things. What she wanted to show us were the windows and the doors. Firstly she showed us the house next door, which was joined to the house on offer. Here, she explained, the new owners were planning to replace the tatty old wooden fixtures with replacements in wood, and we murmured the appropriate sounds of approval. This, as it turned out, was the wrong move. For what she wanted to demonstrate was not the beauty of wood, but the longevity of aluminum.
Her husband, before his death, had had all the wooden fixtures of their house removed and replaced the lot in bright, shiny, modern, character-less aluminum. We made all the right noises and admired the remarkable staying power of this alloy. Installed over thirty years previously there was no sign of wear or decay. It was clear that aluminum was built to last, unlike that old fashioned wooden stuff. She was a real advocate. Indeed some aluminum company would have done well to put her on their staff – on commission of course. She had no maintenance, and she had only to wipe it all over with a soapy cloth every so often keep her fittings looking like new. In the value for money stakes I'm sure that she had come up trumps. But we rather like the idea of watching wood take on individual character as it slowly ages. The idea that the house would always be pristine, with burnished silver colored frames and doors does not appeal to either of us. And we rather enjoy the thought that the wooden shutters will look old fashioned. It was clear that if we were to move in to the square we would have one very disappointed neighbor.

She would be disappointed and confused "Why on earth would they want to put in wood which is sure to rot, when they could have chosen a solution which would last almost for ever?" I could imagine the conversation on the hard wooden chairs that she and her elderly friends occupied on the square, as they marveled once again at the stupidity of the foreigners. We had already decided that this house was not for us, so the aluminum windows did not have to feature in our thought processes. Fortunately I did not have to offend her by explaining why we did not want to choose doors and windows like hers.

Also living around this little square are a handful of widows nick-named by someone the "Barcelona Babes". They are extremely well dressed in fashion wear rather than the traditional black garb of the Spanish widow. I presume that their outfits come from fashionable Barcelona boutiques, rather than the local market. They can be seen taking their *paseo* in the evening. They really look quite incongruous dressed to the nines as they wander along this country road. But clearly they are very happy with life and they seem to live it to the full.

One evening in summer Kathy and I went out for a stroll once the heat of the day had started to subside. We made our first visit back to the square since the day when we had rejected the idea of replacement windows that looked as if they had been fitted by a "nationally recognized" company – the sort that TV consumer shows gets there teeth into. As we wandered through the square it was clear that the house we had visited was still untouched. I don't think that most foreign residents would have wanted somewhere with so little garden attached – and I'm sure that they can't all have been put off by the double-glazing salesman next door.

There was no-body around when we walked through. It was around 9pm, and probably everyone was eating. Certainly one family was doing just that, and they were obviously entertaining guests, because as we walked past one curtained window we heard a very plumy, public school style English voice say in rather over-exaggerated and voluminous tone *"Oh si. Comprende"*. What it was that he understood I do not know, but I think that he may be the chap who so offended our Spanish proponent of aluminum by wasting his energy installing wooden doors and shutters.

We circled the square and satisfied ourselves that we had made the right decision. It is pleasant enough, but we did not want to live in other people's pockets, nor did we want them living in ours. For a little exercise we carried on through to the alternative road out, which joins the main road a few hundred yards further on. At the junction we came upon yet another little old lady laboring away as she husked and laid out the almonds, which had presumably been picked that day. We had a chat, added to our knowledge of the almonding process, and carried on our way.

As we rounded the corner we met up with the "Barcelona Babes". We exchanged greetings and commented on the day. In give-away British style this involved reference to the weather. We then politely took our leave and walked on just a little faster than them. As we turned the next bend we saw one of the many prickly pear cactus plants that grow like weeds around here. I've seen "Jungle Book" so I know about as much about prickly pear as the next man – which is not a lot. I know full well that Baloo used to toss these about and eat them. But neither of us had any idea what the fruit were actually good for.

So I reached out to feel one of them. I had no intention of actually picking one. After all they were not on our land. But just as my hand settled on the plant the "Babes" appeared around the bend and one of the exclaimed *"no par mano".* But it was too late. I had barely touched the fruit, and already the palm and three fingers of my right hand were like a pincushion. I had hundreds of the tiny hairy prickles sticking out of my skin. I smiled sweetly at them – a "thank goodness I wasn't stupid enough to actually touch it" smile. We waved and we carried on home.

Once home I set about trying to extract these tiny barbed hairs. Most of them came out with out problem, but of course enough stayed to really irritate. Kathy proposed a warm bath – always a good suggestion, although I've no idea why. Perhaps it's just that the warmth soothes away the cares and stresses of the day (I should have gone into advertising). But whatever the reason it gave me the excuse I was looking for to use a little of our water supply to further test the spa mechanism in that new bath of ours.

It did the trick. Most of the rest of the prickles eased out, and I felt pleasantly relaxed. Kathy brought me a glass of chilled white wine and I was in seventh heaven. Just then there was a knock on the door. The people from a few doors up the street had come for a drink as arranged. We arranged it – and we forgot all about it. Fortunately Kathy saw them through to the sitting room while I speedily dressed. Our precious water had been able to deliver only a portion of the benefit of which it was capable. But I was feeling relaxed, and we had a very pleasant evening in the company of the locals.

16 – A Home of our Own

Kathy had some clear ideas on what she wanted our house to look like. She collected magazines and kept cuttings. We were both anxious to respect local traditions, and to make full use of local materials. What we had not considered though was the point that things might be done differently here. After all a builder is a builder right? Wrong! Our experience is that the builders we have employed in the UK do things quite differently to Pepé and his gang. The materials here are more traditional, and they are designed for a different climate. But techniques vary too, as does the cost of materials.
I had not considered that the way walls are prepared for plastering would vary greatly. Yet the Spanish team use an enormous quantity of concrete - a special and extremely hard version known as *cemento*. They apply large quantities of the stuff to fill any gaps and smooth out the imperfections. They spread a thick layer on every wall and smooth it fairly level. And only then do they plaster over the top. The plaster, known as *yesso*, is equally hard and very fast drying. The technique to get it to stick is quite something - and getting it up and flat before it dries rock hard is a real challenge. The fact that Spanish builders achieve anything approaching a fairly smooth surface at the end seems something of a miracle. We have now watched several local craftsmen flinging quantities of this concrete mix onto walls. It always looks runny, yet it always seems to stay exactly where they arrange for it to land. They then baton either side of this lumpy mess of gray and run a rod from top to bottom. What remains is a fairly smooth and level surface ready for plastering.
Not only is it smooth and level - it is also incredibly tough. DIYers require really powerful hammer drills to penetrate Spanish walls, and as you might have gathered I am not much cop at doing it myself at the best of times. Kathy describes DIY as "dismantle it yourself" in our house. She's not really being unfair when she says so - a little cruel perhaps, but perfectly fair. So when I came to hang a few pictures, which was about the limit of my handwork, the first thing I had to do was to

borrow a drill that was up to the job. Well it was actually the second thing I had to do, as the first thing I did was to burn out my under-powered bargain acquired for just a few thousand pesetas.
This *yesso* is tough, but I comfort myself with the thought that it makes our house all the stronger. People who know about these things advised us to avoid buying any property without a roof. In the UK you would fear frost damage in the cavity from accumulated rainwater frozen in winter and hence expanding between the bricks. This would cause movement and distortion leading to inevitable damage. Over here frost is only a rare occurrence and normally of the air frost variety. The temperature does not drop low enough to freeze accumulated water. Here the risk is more from temperature changes where heavy falls of rain can be accompanied by sudden switches of heat. The result is evaporation, which in its own way can be as damaging as frost. The other factor to bear in mind is that many "roofless" properties have sat in that state for years. The damage done in that time can be difficult to assess and may well be down in the foundations.
The foundations themselves are another interesting issue - where they exist! Many of these old properties were built directly on the ground, which would have been flattened before construction, but with little other preparation. Even today we have seen dense housing developments being built alongside salt lakes, where the concrete platform laid directly on the cleared fields is the only foundation. The builders presumably rely on the favorable weather to ensure that there is no movement, and being built at roughly sea level there is little chance of the buildings subsiding - I presume. But the scale of the salt lakes has reduced over the years, meaning that many of these developments sit on the salt flats, which once formed the flood planes of these lakes. Climates change, but not always irrevocably in one direction. Who is to say how long it will be before the waters start to rise again? Serious unpredictable rainfall has become an issue in recent years, and a few days of heavy storms could easily re-fill these lakes beyond their capacity. If that happened where, I wonder, would the waters go? On matters of this sort my mind works in simple logical (and often well proven) paths. I reckon there is a jolly good chance that the old "water meadows" are the natural destination. And the effect of that is inevitable - flooded and damaged vacation homes, most of which will be unoccupied at the time because their owners are in the factories of Birmingham or Rotterdam

earning the money to pay the cost of upkeep for their Spanish dream.
Those same mistakes have been made by planners the world over. How often do we read in the papers of rivers bursting their banks, and how often are we told that the incident is just upstream of re-channeling work, or major construction. In answer to the second we are rarely told this – but it is often the truth. We still know very little about the forces of nature, and yet we constantly seem prepared to defy them. Old water meadows have been destroyed all over southern England in the cause of "progress". Industrial estates and business parks now sit on the edges of many of our towns on what would once have been regarded as the river's own land. We assume that we can simply move the course of a river and the waters will do as instructed. And we often ignore the amazing powers of water to find its own channels and to react to change. So frequently we have seen riverbanks reinforced or canalized to ensure smoother flow, only to be followed by flooding up-stream because of restrictions in the works, or downstream because the new increased amount of water is too great for the rest of the river to cope.
I make this point to demonstrate that it is not only Spanish developers who are so naïve as to believe that nature will not touch them – and with many it is greed that gets in the way of logic. So we had our house carefully checked. The roof was in excellent condition, and because the house was in regular use it had been well maintained. The foundations are simple it must be said, but the house is built on the bedrock. This is the reason that our super bubble bath could not be sunken as we had hoped, and its base sits instead only just below the level of the floor. Our house was solid and sound with no signs of damp, or movement – and so far that has proved to be true.
When Pepé and co arrived on site the first thing that they did was to hacksaw through the padlock on the water tank to gain access to our reservoir for mixing concrete, washing down and whatever else it is for which builders require large quantities of water. It is about as mysterious to me as the command from the midwife in those old films to "Boil plenty of water". After all you and I both know that there is little likelihood of the new born infant being asked to drink a cup of tea! But for whatever purpose Pepé saw fit to break into our water tank, and this caused Andréas enormous distress. In May when we were on site he took me on side and told me first what a good job he thought the builders were doing. He told me that we were lucky to have such skilled Spanish craftsmen and he pointed out that the

materials being used were of a fine quality. He then told me how unprofessional they were to break into the reservoir, and how angry they had made him. He, Andréas, held a key to the lock and he was responsible for the safety of the contents. Anything could have been added to our water. How was he to know? And he was our guardian. He was clearly very upset and so next day I was outside the *ferreteria* waiting for them to open in order to buy a new lock with three keys - one for us, one for Andréas and one for Pepé. Our neighbor, my *hombré* made a point of talking sternly to Pepé about the responsibility which had been given to him. He explained that he, Andréas, had to ensure that everything was properly taken care of in our absence and that he would carefully monitor any sign of abuse of the privilege that we had bestowed upon this poor builder. Fortunately Pepé is a stoical sort. He said "yes" and "no" respectfully and in all the right places - and then carried on as before.

A few weeks after we first saw *Cortijo Oliverico*, the house that was destined not to be ours, we found ourselves in a local artists' exhibition in a neighboring Hampshire village. Our friend Keith Chapman is no mean artist himself and he had invited us to the pre-public viewing of the Wallop Artist annual exhibition. Now we went along out of curiosity more than with any intent to buy. But good intent often falls at the first hurdle, and our first hurdle was the glass of wine that Keith gave to each of us on arrival. They're no fools these artists. The second hurdle was strategically positioned just ahead of us in the form of a spectacular acrylic painting of a Provencal house. The outstanding colors of the Mediterranean sun set off the creamy stonework at dusk. The bright yellows, the orange and shades of red were startling and we knew immediately that set against a plain white wall this picture would be stunning. Having weakened we looked further and that day we spend a few bob on several unique pieces by artists from our home in England to grace the walls of our home in Spain. Those that were not already framed Kathy took to our neighbor Bill, who is a renowned specialist in the field, and we loaded them into the car at Easter to transport them all out to Almería.

We were very lucky because a colleague agreed to swap his Ford Galaxy "people mover" for my car for 2 weeks or so. This meant that Kathy and I could load up the back with all the bits and pieces we could fit. The van of our journey down there was quickly converted back into a six-seater car for travelling around with Kathy's parents and the boys, who had flown on ahead. Over the six or eight months since we first committed to this

corner of Spain I had accumulated all sorts of things that would look "just right" in our new home.
I cannot deny that my greatest extravagance was the candles. In Winchester there seemed to be a steady flow of special offers on candles and wrought iron stands. We bought a large flat, birthday cake sized, candle with 5 wicks, which sits on a flat, plate shaped iron dish. That was intended to sit in the middle of the dining table, which we knew we would eventually buy, even if we had no idea what sort of table it might be. But the ones that enthused me most are two candles each around 6 inches in diameter, standing in wrought Iron holders that sit on the floor. Each has three wicks and one is three feet tall, while the other is 5 feet. Whether I will ever have the nerve to light them I can't be sure. They look so marvelous in their virginal state. But they now stand in corners, the short one in the sitting room with church style candles of various heights alongside. The tall candle is in the dining room and greets everyone who walks the length of the room from the front door into the kitchen or the sitting room.
The dining table of which we are both so proud was not really the right place for the candle bought specially for the job. So instead it now sits on a coffee table made of re-claimed pine and bought on Winchester market. Mind you when Andréas told me that he hadn't seen such large candles outside a church, I think he began to wonder what we might be up to. One look at our glass topped dining table, mounted on those marble and stone pillars and he knew that his new neighbors must be mad. He explained to me very painstakingly in slow over-emphasized Spanish, and with his croaking voice more pronounced than ever, that this was a foolish thing for us to have done. He explained in worried terms that "*El cristal es muy peligroso*". He had obviously not seen all those *Casa y Cocina* magazines that Kathy had studied so hard to improve her Spanish. There was no convincing him. He knew that glass is very dangerous and that was that.
He even took me down the drive to visit his brother's house, next door to his own. This particular sibling is one of the non-resident property owners who live in Barcelona. He returns in summer I was told – and this was August! But I was not here to learn more about Andréas family tree. No I was here to see what a dining table should look like. It was becoming increasingly clear that we should have had the village carpenter produce a good solid pine table, square cut with no fancy bits. Together with the table there should be six hard as rocks flat-seated pine chairs. Considering that Spanish families seem to live around the dining

table when they're not working or watching the television out in the street I could not understand why they have to make the chairs on which they sit so darned uncomfortable. I imagine that this is why Spaniards in bars lean so heavily on the tables. It must be partly to support them following the effects of alcohol, and partly to ease the pressure on their rear ends.

Andréas may not understand our design ideas, but that table, the candles and our selection of art have helped to turn the modest little house we bought into *La Higuera* – a home of our own.

17 - Las Ramblas

Barcelona is my favorite city for a number of reasons. I love the *Plaza Catalonia*, the grand square dominated by the great department store, *El Corte Ingles*. I was honored to be invited to the "topping out" ceremony for the Olympic Village, prior to the 1992 games. We visited the renewed stadium and studied the views from the imposing position up on the *Mont Juic*. This magnificent hill is just one of the five which surround Barcelona and can be reached by road or via the *Teleferico*. This cable car travels high across the seaport of Barcelona from *Barceloneta* to the mountain, which houses the city's famous stadium.

I love the people of Barcelona. They are both sophisticated and welcoming at the same time. They have all the style of the Milanese or the Parisians, but without the same degree of clutter as Milan or the arrogance of Paris. Barcelona has some superb restaurants, catering for traditional local taste as well as for the very broadest of international palates. I have had excellent haute cuisine, superb *tapas*, country style roast boar and even a very good curry here. Add to all that the good value for money and the sunshine and this is a most attractive city.

But the bit of Barcelona that the world knows best must be the *Rambla.* The direct translation is an avenue, and in Barcelona this is exactly what you get, a wide continental boulevard, lined with mature trees. Down the middle runs a wide reservation, which houses cafes and bars, newsagent's kiosks and even a bird market. It is quite normal to see exhibitions of good quality art being offered at reasonable prices, and the city opera house is located half way down. I was fortunate in seeing a performance of *La Cinerentola* just a few weeks before the fire, which gutted the place. It was a magnificent building and has now been lovingly restored to re-establish it as one of the fine opera houses of Europe.

The *Plaza Espana* is situated to one side. And the harbor is at the opposite end from the *Plaza Catalonia.* This avenue is the very heart of Barcelona for many tourists. Though I know that the city has so much more to offer, especially the most wonderful displays of architecture, I really do enjoy sitting in a bar on *Las*

Ramblas with a beer in front of me as I watch the world go by. Here they have the common sense to provide comfortable chairs in which you can relax over a leisurely drink as a wide variety of humanity passes. A few of them drag their yappy little dogs behind them – these I can do without.
In the country, and especially in the south, the *ramblas* have another significance. Still wide, they are there to carry the floodwaters on the rare occasions when heavy rains arrive. It seems that here man works with nature to manage the water flows. But this has been achieved by letting the waters dictate their own course. These wide dried riverbeds flow from the mountains towards river valleys and the sea. They take fairly direct routes, and where human intervention has strengthened their sides or widened the channels our forbears learned some time ago that the direction chosen by the waters is very difficult to change.
This is how our village comes to have a *rambla* cross the road at either end of the village. The hills on which our house is built run to the west of the road, with a natural valley to the east. Further north and south the position is reversed as the road picks its way between the hills. The result is that the flood channel changes its position relative to the road in several places. And when the floods come with a vengeance the village can be cut off. A few months before our first visit the rains had been torrential. The first heavy rains for several years, and the *rambla* filled from dust flats to fast flowing river overnight. Even when the weathermen on television forecast rain no one believes that they mean real rain. In fact I can picture Apollonia in her hostal shouting at the set that the forecaster doesn't know what he is talking about. Just occasionally though they get it right, and when it really rains it really really rains.
But nature has prepared. These watercourses carry millions of gallons of water away in an orderly fashion and at rapid speed. The problem comes for communities like ours, for which there is only one road passing through the village. That year the village was cut off for three days and nights. The village bakery ran out of flour and the shop did business like it had never done before.
Many people resorted to raiding the freezers to find long forgotten packets of something unrecognisable, and old Felipé in one of the neighboring villages settled back to do what he does best. And what he does best is to get extremely drunk at someone else's expense. In the process he drank many litres of strong rough red wine. No one was too sure of the origin, and no one was too worried about the cost. The effect that everyone

dreads when he goes on a binge is on his digestive system, which turns into a major scale methane plant. The area for several feet around him is turned toxic at regular intervals, and often there is no let up at all between one burst and another.
He eats large quantities of the greasiest *jamon* and sings numerous unrecognizable local folk songs. But things always turn for the worst when he gets amorous. It lasts for only a couple of hours, and is the pre-cursor to total oblivion for half a day or so. Those two hours can be hell for the people at the receiving end though – and he's not usually too picky on who they might be. Amour and methane are not a good combination, add those two to an inability to stand or speak coherently and you start to understand the problem.
Fortunately for the people of our village he was a few miles away and cut off by the floods. The effects of his excesses were therefore restricted to his own village, where the locals took it in turns to try to restrain him. They knew from years of experience that after those few hours of drunken flirtation he would collapse in a heap somewhere and sleep a long sleep. The task then is to ensure that he sleeps safely. That is to say not in the path of the floodwaters, not in the path of the goatherd and not in a position where asphyxiation might come before wakefulness. They succeeded this time as most others. And after a day and a night of smelly peace he awoke, as always with a raging thirst and a bit of a headache, but otherwise as right as rain. He asked the same questions he always asked – "Who covered my clothes in this mess?" " Why is she looking at me like that?" and "What on earth is that awful smell?"
Other villages had a much calmer time. Village bars did roaring trade, and in one case managed to bring in more beer by sending the best tractor in the village with large trailer attached to scale the hills and find a way through to an open road. It took the best part of a day, but they did it. The *patróns* of the two competing bars pooled their resources and shared the investment. They also shared the decision to nearly double their prices. "Well this is a crisis," one of them said. When asked where was his generous spirit he replied that it was in bottles and on sale at the present very "favorable" prices. They had apparently judged things well, as for the next couple of days business boomed. It flagged dramatically though once the water level dropped, and in almost direct relation.
The various local *ramblas* come together in nearby and flow, or more accurately don't flow for most of the time, into the *Almanzora* River just south of the town. Our local town is split in

two by the rambla. A majestic bridge spans the gap created and joins the two halves together. Most locals though use the bed of the flood way itself to access the other side. There are slip roads and lanes running along the two sides, and the whole thing has been turned from what must once have been a casual cut from one community to the other into a formal arrangement of access and priority.

The parking problems in town and the need to leave space for all the learner drivers have led to a fairly formal use of the *rambla* as the main public car park. As the flow of traffic across needs to be protected in various places there is an order about this parking, which is really quite uncommon over here. Disorder reigns though once a week on market day when the main town squares are overrun with market stalls and crowds of shoppers. The stalls, the cars and the shoppers spill down into the *rambla* where the livestock traders, a few fruit and vegetable stalls and the cabinetmakers ply their trade.

The whole town comes alive on market day, and the *rambla* is a vital part of that life. Old boys stand under the bridge to benefit from the shade and chatter about the things that old men discuss with one another. The widows dressed in black stagger under the weight of their shopping to get back to the pre-arranged meeting point, to catch the lift arranged with son or neighbor. The songbirds in cages sing their plaintive songs and the various motorized vehicles move around raising both temperature and tempers.

There are a number of local groups who meet to share their hobbies. One of these is an international group of walkers, who, understandably I regret, have chosen to call themselves the *Ramblas.* These ramblers meet regularly to share the pleasure of walking the hills hereabout and I imagine that they usually finish off in a local hostelry. When I say finish off that might be Freudian slip, as I am sure that their exertions would finish me off. And when I say a local hostelry it is mainly because I know darned well that that's where I would want to end up to give me a chance of recovery.

But even their exertions are put to shame by the devoted local church people. They parade up the *rambla* once a year to carry the statue of the Virgin from the central Church in Albox, all the 12 or so miles up to the sanctuary nearly 5000 feet above sea level. For the early part of this walk the gradient rises slightly and the walk to even a few miles north of our village is not too grueling. But here things start to get serious. The road winds its

way up the cliff side and travels long distances to make any real progress just because of the need to climb.
Albox is around 1300 feet above sea level. We two thirds of the way to this peak are about 2500 feet, and in the final third of the distance the height increases by a further 2500 feet. And what these devotees carry is no papier-mâché replica. It is a seventeenth century sculpture by Alfonso de Mena, which although only 2 feet tall weighs a good few pounds. The Virgin is defended by two angelic creatures and she wears a large halo. The statue is distinctly baroque, carved in *sabina* wood, and it stands on a replacement silver plinth made in the factory of famous goldsmith Miguel Moreno.
So this procession, which happens in September, involves the transportation of a valuable, delicately balanced, heavy and difficult to carry religious icon, along an unmade track. There are boulders and other debris along the way, which rises gently during the part of the journey when energy is at its greatest and very steeply when stamina is at its lowest. And this happens every year. Local businesses close for this *fiesta* day, and many many people make the journey. Some walk the whole distance, others just a part. But these are a devout people and they make this journey because it is a pilgrimage. They regard it as a privilege to be fit and able to take part and they thank God for another opportunity.
We say our thanks too, because our home looks down the valley and the rambla passes just below us. This was the only roadway at one time, long before solid road surfaces were constructed. In those days the watercourses were the major communication tracks, and, so long as the rains did not come, the *ramblas* provided donkey tracks linking together the various communities. Today there are still many hamlets that rely on the *ramblas* for access, and when the rains come no one else either comes or goes.
They are not a very pretty roadway. They are unmade, and are often used as a dump for all sorts of unwanted bits and pieces from garden debris to the occasional twin tub. The new local council has declared war on fly tipping and a major clear up is in hand. Some of the locals find this rather unnecessary, as they have lived with the intermittent debris for as long as they can remember. The newcomers on the other hand have a different perspective. And as newcomers always do they try to change things. So the new mayor has the full support of the foreigners who have moved in, and by dint of that the support of those villagers who would like to cash in their assets by selling on the

family home to "wealthy" foreigners. What they may never appreciate is that many of these so called wealthy are here only because there are properties to be had for less than a small deposit on a house at home.
Those are the properties that need real money spent on them to make them habitable. They are the ones that are located next to the neighbors pig-sty (ok I admit if you like that sort of thing) and they are the ones that are in the most inaccessible places. Three miles up the *rambla* for example!

18 – It's Round Here Somewhere

I have a remarkable nose for finding my way around. Years ago, on vacation in Corfu, we were joined for a week by Kathy's parents. They had visited the island the year before, and as it was our first visit they kind of took us under their wings and showed us around. One of the first places they took us to was a fabulous patisserie in the centre of Corfu town. It was down various back streets and not so easy to find. A few days later we visited the other end of the island, as I wanted to explore a new property, which my company planned to feature in the following year's summer brochure. The hotel was everything I had been led to expect, and we returned to our hotel via Corfu town feeling rather pleased with things. We approached from the opposite direction and despite the unfamiliar town and the maze of small streets I drove directly to the cake shop to my mother in law's undying amazement.

I have to say that I can't claim the same success in Brussels, but as this is an absolute exception I am convinced that it is the layout and lack of design in Brussels, rather than any personal shortcoming, that is to blame. I have driven in Paris, Athens, Madrid and even New York with no problems. I am very good at finding my way around. In Brussels though I fail on 1 trip in 2. I always get to the target eventually, but it often requires me to re-trace a previous taxi journey or two, rather than use my in-built compass to find my way directly.

I have seen some of the most interesting parts of Brussels, and found myself locking all the doors as I have found myself driving through the red light district behind the Gare du Nord, when I thought I was nearing the Grand Place. And I assure you that nothing, least of all the women sitting in the display windows there, would entice me to the red light district unless it were the only route to my destination.

Over here I have had very few problems finding my way around. I have been driving in Spain on occasions for nearly thirty years. There are few of the well-known parts of Spain in which I have

not driven at some point, and with few difficulties. Spain is well sign-posted, and the road network has been substantially upgraded over the last few years. So I pride myself on finding my way rather well. It was therefore something of a personal slight that I could not find several of the local facilities, especially when I had been so well directed.
On our second visit to the area, and while staying with Apollonia we met a guy called Dave. It seems that he had been something in advertising, and we found out that we had a few business acquaintances in common. We were talking about shopping locally and he directed us to the "big" local store, Hiper Olé. He made clear that it is on the Baza road, heading west out of Albox. Not far past the ITV he told me – I swear. Everyone knows where the ITV is in every locality. It is the local, state owned, vehicle testing centre. Every car over 4 years old must be check, or controlled as our continental cousins have it, each year. The local ITV is around 6 miles west of the town.
We headed off next morning, as I like to get a handle on things as soon as possible. We drove west and eventually drove past the industrial estate that houses the ITV. It also accommodates various marble showrooms, garages, distribution centers and the like. We carried on as instructed and after several more miles we passed the turning to Catral. A few miles further on and I realized that we had driven nearly as far past the ITV as we had driven to reach it, and we gave up. It was obvious to me that we had been badly directed. This chap clearly didn't know what he was talking about – or perhaps we had been influenced by the (small) amount of alcohol consumed the night before. As if!
I told Dave that he was perhaps confused when he gave his directions, but he was adamant that he had been both accurate and correct, so I decided to give the benefit of the doubt in my intention of proving that I was not stupid. So we drove off again in a westerly direction as my friends from the boys in blue might put it. We passed the ITV and the marble showrooms, and we passed the Catral junction. Shortly after the bend we approached the Macael junction, and there below us on the left, as bold as brass was Hiper Olé. It was clearly signed and had flags to make it easier to find. We just hadn't been patient enough to keep going until we found it.
Having given up on it the first time we had turned our heels and headed east, passing Albox en route. We found an alternative shop called Piman. This amazing little warehouse stocks all the usual food and household items, plus a few of the more unusual. You know the sort of thing, a jackhammer, or a cement mixer. In

the country folk do not like to waste their time running from store to store. So, as Pablo explains it to me, he can satisfy his wife Maria, by taking her to Piman to do the weekly shop, while he visits the adjoining building and DIY section. They stock every kind of tool and fitting you can imagine, and I have to say, DIYer or not, I am fascinated by it all. How on earth do the people who do these things know that they need a 10mm wood bit, or a self-adjusting chuck - and how do they know what they are any way? I think that I may be a Pimanoholic if such an animal exists. Piman is untidy and disorganized. Most of the staff seem to have no more than a scant knowledge of what they stock - and even less idea of what their various merchandise does.
This is only one example of the difficulty I seem to meet when finding the most ordinary places. One of the main products of this area is almonds, and the cooperative, which processes, sorts, grades and packs them in located close to the centre of town. "It's easy to find," said Max "just behind the BP garage." And he was right. It was there bold as brass, exactly where he told me. So now I knew that I had found my feet I decided to go for the pair. The other major agricultural product is olives, and on the day when we first saw La Higuera we called in to the annual food fair. There we saw all sorts of goodies from around Almería and Andalucía, including Almanzora Valley olive oil. We were given a tasting on a piece of the wonderful local bread, and of course we just had to take a bottle home with us.
Having discovered this nectar we spent bits of subsequent visits looking for the oil in the local shops. We were offered every other brand and were given very strange looks - but nowhere did we find the local oil. So back I went to Max and asked him for directions. But directions came there none. He did not know where the oil comes from and could not tell us where the locally grown olives are taken to be pressed. Keith and Vicki knew that the local presses are in a warehouse on an industrial estate opposite the ITV. Sound familiar? They had not actually been there themselves but assumed that it would be easy to find. It was not! Kathy and I went twice. We drove around the whole area, even heading into the hills. But on neither visit did we find a single suggestion that olives were pressed in the area.
I asked at the local Michelin dealer who looked at me as if I had just arrived from Mars. We called on an unmarked warehouse, where we found four or five very greasy looking chaps who might well have been assembling the next moon orbiter, or bombs for ETA for all I knew. They certainly did not press olives, but told me that I could get oil just a couple of doors away. And this is

how I came to be negotiating for a gallon of used engine oil freshly out of the sump. Once I had the chance to see what was on offer I soon explained my mistake. What a laugh we could have shared with the mechanic if only he had not taken exception to my obviously planned waste of his time. We gave up.

As we had not been through an olive harvest we had no idea what destiny was planned for the fruit, but in December, as harvest approached, the situation became clearer. Vicki and Keith had just returned from a trip back to England as we arrived, and as gifts had taken various of their own produce, including olive oil from the local co-operative. It was the very co-operative that produces the Almanzora Valley oil, and Keith was able to confirm that it is indeed right opposite the ITV. He and Vicki described it to us and offered to take us there. I, as you now know, am severely independent and am also hampered by impatience. So we asked them to talk us through the directions one more time.

Vicki explained that if we were to take the minor turning directly opposite the ITV we would be no more than 200 yards away, but that to get there we would need to continue to the proper junction and look for the marble works. The presses are in an industrial unit just beyond it seemed. And to help she told me to look for the diamond cutting wheel on display outside the unit in front. So, never one to assume that the other person is entirely correct, I took the minor junction and drove 200 yards in the only direction possible. Here we were driving behind the large marble works – we must be in the right area. Not surprisingly we were not. We went to the smaller units and started asking around once again. I hoped that I would not be recognized, or that new and more knowledgeable staff would now be employed. I was offered directions to the engine oil re-processing centre – an offer that I politely refused, and eventually, after receiving directions from the same Michelin centre we headed back to the slip road from the proper junction and turned left. Ahead of us was a dead end, blocked by bushes, beyond which was that little turning which I had taken in my own impulsive way. We knew that this could not be right, but then noticed that on our left was a diamond cutter specialist. Their display outside this little factory unit was a couple of large replica diamond cutting wheels.

We were close, but where to now. I backed up and headed off behind the cutter factory. There was an unmarked unit, which we had missed completely on our previous visits. The aroma was pungent, and as we turned in we met an enormous open lorry on its way out loaded with pulped olives. The pigs round here live on a very rich diet following the olive harvest. What it does for their digestion I hate to think. Inside the little office the man I take to be the manager remembered us from the food fair over a year before and took us through the pressing rooms to show off his operation. Our olives now swell his stocks by the most miniscule amount, but on that day we drove off with a couple of gallon containers filled with his produce. We boosted his pride and we added just a little to his coffers. Our purchases found their way to various friends elsewhere in Spain and to friends and colleagues in England and in other parts of northern Europe. If only we had found it on the previous visit when we had the "people mover" with us. Explaining these large containers of olive oil at Alicante Airport check-in was a trifle tricky.

We have only made it into Almería city once in this first year. It was a wet day and we decided that as well as seeing the culture we might also visit the shopping facilities. No I'm sorry I must have this right - I decided to look at the architecture, which Kathy also enjoyed, but she decided that having driven so far to a minor metropolis it would be a terrible waste not to part with some money. We had been told about the major new shopping centre on the road in from the highway. As we approached the city centre the signs were everywhere. So clearly this would be easy to find on our way home. It was not.

After enjoying the culture of the city centre (and a jolly good lunch) we left by the exact same road and did not see a single billboard. We checked at every junction, and we asked various knowledgeable (and local) looking pedestrians. This was all without success. I did the obvious and headed out far enough to turn round towards the centre so that we might re-find the hoardings we had seen on the way in and follow their directions. We tried - oh how we tried - but with no success. We found ourselves in a high-rise housing estate surrounded by bored young Almerians. Having escaped from here we ended up in schoolyard and later in the loading bay of a local factory, surrounded by hooting and very high-articulated lorries. At this point I gave up on the search and I think that Kathy was close to giving up on me.

I did the obvious. I asked her what it was she had wanted to buy, and before she explained that she wanted to "browse" I announced that we could get everything we needed in our local Piman store. We did, all except the adapter for the hose, which I needed to attach an extension. I knew they had them, I'd seen them there before. But neither I nor the staff on duty could find them. I eventually left saying "it really was not at all important" as the more senior of the staff headed off into the electrical section muttering something along the lines of "It must be round here somewhere."

19 - Getting Around

Not so many years ago the local communities were lost in the hills. The only visitors were buying marble, or were the normal itinerant tradesmen. It lulled into tranquillity after the Moors departed and for some time nothing much happened here at all. The roads were lousy and today many locals should be grateful that it took so long for the town to wake up, because otherwise the strangers who have changed so much of Europe as they travel around would doubtless have ruined this spot too. Huercal Overa to the East and Baza to the west were connected by a quiet and windy main road. It passed through all the towns and villages on the way and drivers would allow a day to make the journey that today takes around an hour.

This was the only surfaced road until the second half of the century when a few of the mountain roads were formalized and roads were built alongside some of the *ramblas*. The growing marble industry demanded transport, which these roads could not provide and the livestock market in Baza was developing as the main centre for agricultural business in Eastern Andalucía, attracting farmers and dealers from as far away as Granada and Murcia. Better access was needed and a busy single-track railway line was built to connect Baza with Almería, Huercal Overa, and Vera travelling past the towns of Albox, Arboleas and Cantoria. This branch line to the southeast was de-commissioned some time ago.

As in England, when Dr Beaching cut the rail network at a stroke in the 1960s, it was the development of the road network that was to mark the end of the railway as a viable freight transportation system in the rural areas over here. The old Spanish line still exists for almost its complete length, rusting, alongside the road, which is under almost constant improvement. Many of the old halts and stations are still there, and some of them sit uneasily next to roundabouts or flyovers. The line has only been broken in the few places where modern expedience has allowed a new junction on the main road to slice the line in two. At Ollula del Rio, just by that supermarket which we had so much trouble finding, there is a smart new junction of motorway

standards, and the locals are proud that their community requires such an important connection with the outside world.
This new section of road has created a grand by pass around the little town and given it a whole new status. But I am sure that the builders miss the irony that this impressive new stretch of road with its flyover and slip roads was made possible only by slicing away a piece of the old railway line. Only around 150 yards had to be sacrificed to make way for the new road, but that is enough and is perfectly positioned to ensure that the railway could not be re-connected without removing or re-routing the expensive new road that replaced it. The whole irony is symbolized by the old Ollula del Rio station, which drivers must pass as they take the slip road up onto the highway heading for Albox. It stands there in decay, and doubtless will do so for years to come. At some point in the future local people will look back on the closure of the railway with regret. Even more they will lament the decision to dismantle enough of it to make its re-opening virtually impossible. They will point out that this happened at the very time that in northern Europe railways were being re-opened and new lines built to encourage freight to leave the roads for environmental and valid economic reasons.
At a time when successive British governments have failed to invest in transport systems and milked the motorist for all they can get, the Spanish government has been very canny. When we first traveled to Spain by car in the early 1980s the coastal motorway, which now follows the Mediterranean coast, was far from complete. I well remember being asked to comment in the UK press on yet another fatal accident on the infamous "death row", the coast road south from Malaga. This stretch was perhaps the worst, but the quality of other sections of road was far from perfect. In 1986 we took the ferry from Plymouth to Santander and arrived on Spanish soil relaxed and refreshed. The roads system though was set on upsetting that sense of ease in just a few short hours.
Santander was a pretty little harbor on the northern coast. It opens out towards the Bay of Biscay and has a fine fishing tradition that goes back many centuries. The local produce was then transported overland to the major markets in central and southern Spain. The overland connection used also to be by train, and many traders preferred to get their produce to the southern cities by means of freight ships, which plied their trade from Bilbao and Santander to Cadiz and the Mediterranean ports. The reason for this option was the magnificent Picos mountain range. The Picos are an outstanding range of peaks. They are as

green as the summer Alps and house Spain's major dairy production. They are, though, very rural and the road system which existed in the late 1980s was not designed with major freight transportation in mind. Neither did it easily carry the shipload of cars and lorries that disgorged a couple of times each week.

For some of the passengers and drivers the slow ambling way of the Picos was the very reason for catching the ferry to Santander. For those of us anxious to reach destinations in the south in a reasonable time they were a beautiful interlude, but one heck of a handicap. Just as in Almería the mountain roads wound through various passes and villages and the livestock being moved from one pasture to another, or from field to dairy, created a stress inducing mixture of hazard and delay.

Until the passing of Franco, *El Generalisimo,* Spain was not encouraged to get too close to the outside world. With the exception of Portugal, itself at the end of a long period of central control, Spain was protected from the rest of the world by mountains and seas. Franco restricted his investment to domestic needs, and then controlled expenditure to the point that the peasant society in rural Spain was worthy of a developing nation. Since democracy returned so too has investment and Spain now boasts one of the healthiest and fastest growing economies in Europe. This has required and led to an ever-closer relationship in Europe and around the world – especially the Spanish-speaking world.

Spain and Portugal quickly took advantage of the opportunity to join an expanding European Union, with none of the breast beating of the British or certain of the Scandinavians. Spain was welcomed with and discovered an amazing array of gifts. There were tax concessions and beneficial loans, but far more importantly there were the central funds, and there were grants. The central funds, principally the Common Agricultural Fund, were important because Spain was from the start a net beneficiary. This has enabled Spain to invest heavily in her existing agricultural infrastructure, and to build whole new industries. It is thanks to this finance that Almería is now the greenhouse of Europe, producing industrial quantities of the best fruits, salads and vegetables around.

The grants were to help re-build the Spanish infrastructure and along with the hard work of her people to make Spain the economic powerhouse it is today. Even on that drive in the mid-eighties we passed sections of road under construction or development, and each bore proudly the symbol of the Spanish interior department and the blue flag with yellow stars of the European Union. These signs announced that this was another development project of the state funded by the European Union. That road-building program has created a most impressive collection of motorways, or motorway standard roads the length and breadth of Spain.

When we made that first journey via Santander it took us 12 hours to reach our destination. Today we can make that same journey in less than 9. It does not pass through as much mountain greenery as it did in the past, but unless that is your objective, and for most of us it is not, then a fast and trouble free journey will be the aim. I regularly face the M3 or M25 and still wonder at the British ability to create and maintain daily gridlock. Why oh why must we encourage drivers to sit nose to tail spewing out vast quantities of noxious gasses. Could it be to allow the government to collect such large sums as they require to fund the other activities of administration and to build up the treasure chest, which now seems mandatory to enable pre-election tax handouts?

If they would only comprehend the impossibility of creating an acceptable transport system without investment and re-direct some of the cash they receive to provide a suitable balance of roads and railways, enabling both public transport and private motoring to combine into a system of choice. Every major journey should provide the traveler with sensible options and combinations, which will over time encourage more of us to make more of our journeys in a vehicle other than our own. Here in Almería there is little public transport, but our time here requires us to do little travelling. The weekly market provides what the land and our neighbors do not and the computer modem means that the whole world is available when we want it and on our terms in our own home, Telefonica permitting. It is possible to do a day's work here and to achieve so much more. The telephone keeps us in touch and E-mail, the curse of the modern office, means that messages are almost instantly received. Comments can be sought and provided, text and designs can be reviewed and revised, and all without ever having to enter one of those soulless office blocks that fill every major city today.

The little white vans are the only regular cause of traffic hold ups hereabouts. Goats come a close second and elderly village folk chatting into car windows in the middle of the road also make their mark. But to my way of thinking the most worrying trend is the slowly rising population of two seater vehicles, which can legally operate without any form of license. I am told that this invention is entirely the responsibility of the French. There is an increasing number of nationals of France, who for one reason or another are not legally entitled to drive a full size car. The law traditionally allows them to drive low powered alternatives, intended, as in the UK, to cover such vehicles as motorized bicycles. In Britain we allow learner motorcyclists to drive three wheelers, and this was the making of Reliant in the sixties. But the British system was tightened up to require provisional motorcycle license holders to take formally recognized instruction and to sit tests after certain periods. This and the comedian Jasper Carrot's regular jibes at the "Robin Reliant" somehow took away the glamour for the youth who were once Reliant's market.

In France an alternative vehicle has been developed, a four-wheeler, two seater, this requires neither tax, nor driver's license. The vehicle must be registered, presumably so that the victim can be identified when run over by a real car, but beyond this nothing much is required. I hear with horror that these vehicles are to be introduced onto the UK's roads by none other than the Reliant Motor Company of A5 fame. I am not sure what rules will apply in Britain, but in Spain, as in France, they are available to anyone with little formality, except that the purchasers can afford them. In fact they are demonstrated at every town fair and are even on offer at the weekly markets in the area. Over here the target market is anyone who would not qualify to drive a real car. While the young test failures are unlikely ever to be seen dead in one, the potential for convicted drink drivers and the like to get mobile once again is a frightening thought.

In fact though most are driven by the older members of our population, who have not driven anything for sometime, or who feel it is time to hang up the keys to the little white van once and for all. It concerns me that anyone who feels unsafe in a solid little van should feel any safer in one of these. The distance between the back bumper and the back of your head is counted in inches rather than feet, and the front bumper is around the same distance from your feet. It worries me even more as I watch them struggle to maneuver out of the Rambla on market day, driving their new motor for the first time. Their faces display the nerves and abject horror of a granny on a Disneyland roller coaster for the first time. The difference is that she will get off after a few minutes, and will probably vow never to do anything so foolish again. These newly emancipated motorists will keep at it until they get the hang of it – or they accept they will keep

driving even though they do not really understand what is happening around them.
These little vehicles have the added danger that they look a little like cars. At least the bubble cars of the 1950s and 60s had the decency not to pretend to be anything other than a real fun way of getting around. Today the whole power thing has moved up to such a degree that anything that looks like a car will lead the drivers of modern and powerful vehicles to assume that they can stop and move like any other car. The same cannot be said for the road riding rotavator. These bits of farmyard equipment are cleverly, if dangerously, converted to allow the landowner to add a trailer behind and move produce, feed, fertilizer and the like around his "estate" as the need demands. Being canny souls they have extended the territory and often run to a neighbor's farm, or into the market astride these most uncomfortable looking bits of kit. The basic equipment is a cultivator of the ride on variety. The domestic walk behind type simply will not do. The rear end of the devise is hooked over the hitching point of a double axle trailer, thus raising the dangerous bit (the blades) off the ground. The engine powers the front axle of the cultivator and the blades are disengaged. This provides the motive force to head off, trailer in tow, to move whatever must be moved on and around the farm.
I was surprised when I first saw two of these make shift vehicles heading off down the Rambla one market day. I was dismayed when I saw one cleaned and polished in a wedding procession heading past our house towards the local church. The owner and (I presume) his wife were perched up front, dressed in their Sunday best. On the trailer behind were six younger members of the family. I imagine that it was his son or daughter plus spouse and offspring. There they sat precariously as they bumped along. As they were a part of the procession, which returned into town around 2 hours later, I can only imagine that they made it both there and back. By the following morning I imagine that their backs shoulders and knees were all aching from hanging on and being bounced around. It may not be my idea of wedding transport, but I suppose it is one way of getting around.

20 - Fiestas and Ferias

We British tend to celebrate in a rather reserved sort of a way. I went to two of the key matches in a recent rugby world cup. In the first England beat Italy by a stonking margin, but by the second the England team had been knocked out in a well-fought game with New Zealand. New Zealand went on to come fourth, and even failed automatic qualification to take part in the next series, which take place in their own country. That's the sort of thing that we seem to do well in sport these days. We may not have failed automatic qualification for a tournament that we will host. But at least we lost to the side that did.

The second game that I saw in Twickenham was the Australia – South Africa semi-final. I invited two Australian along to join our party. Ted is a great rugby man, and I swear he put all of himself into every point scored by his national side. Barry also jumped and shouted at the appropriate times and my fellow British colleagues and I showed our excitement in normal style by commenting to those seated alongside what a good pass or score we had just seen. The game was a real nail-biter, especially towards the end and I was so mesmerized by the action and engrossed in the game that I sat glued to my seat and moved as little as possible. I obviously didn't want to miss any of the action by moving about or, worse still, making a noise.

You get the point I'm sure, and so it is with all celebrations. When the Brits do let our hair down we tend to do so after copious quantities of lager and require the controlling hand of the boys in blue. Our big celebrations, royal jubilees or victory days are organized events with a job for everyone and ordered rows of tables and chairs. Someone is always in charge and the children are the main focus of the festivities with jelly and tinned salmon sandwiches. Although today it is more likely to be quiche or pizza and tarte tatin – very British!

The latin nations, by contrast, throw themselves into celebration at every opportunity. The children are at the heart of Spanish society, here they are treated as fully paid up members of that society, not as a special group who must be pandered before the adults can tuck them up safely in bed. Parents and grandparents will only then go off and party adult style. Cockneys can still lay on a good old knees up and working people everywhere know how to enjoy themselves, but there is always a certain reserve. It is almost as if there is something just a little uncouth in public celebration unless it is orderly and controlled. We do let our hair down, but only so far and only for so long.

Younger generations have experienced the effects of alcohol and sunshine combined and try to replicate them in their parties at home. A wet English industrial suburb will never replicate the atmosphere of a Mediterranean sun spot. Perhaps the sunshine has something to do with it all, but whatever the cause the fact of the matter is that our Mediterranean cousins are much better at partying than we are. Five or six years ago we drove back through Spain to catch the Portsmouth ferry from Bilbao. We arrived the night before and spent the night in an inexpensive hostal in a nearby fishing town called Castro Urdeales. It serves as a rather chilly northern seaside resort, a little like paddling along the Atlantic coast. But the town still thrives on the local fishing fleet. We thoroughly enjoyed wandering around and exploring the castle and the numerous mediaeval buildings, and as we strode along the front we came upon the fish market where a few women were helping the men to set up tables and chairs.

This was to be a celebration of the harvest, which these brave men bring home all year in their little boats and tonight they, their families and anyone else who happened to live nearby, or even pass by would party in style. There wasn't a karaoke machine in sight, and no one had needed to visit Safeway or the local equivalent to stock up. We were invited to join them all and we jumped at the opportunity.

The coals were lit at around 7pm, but no cooking started until after 9 o'clock. Mark had wandered off meantime and settled to watch the sunset from the castle headland and Paul had disappeared several times to check on the barbecue and to see what was on offer. Here we had a potential problem, as he is not too keen on fish. He was persuaded though to try the swordfish steaks rather than the sardines and as the gas lamps were lit we shared the local fish, bread, wine and salad. The music was provided by a local guitar band, which played flamenco and other traditional styles. This was one of the best parties that I have ever been invited to, there was revelry into the early hours and everyone had fun. No one tried to "keep the noise down", and many of the fishermen and their wives sang or danced. And they did so because they were joyful. There was no attempt to put on a show. These people just enjoyed giving thanks with all the joy that their hearts could muster.

And so it is in Almería, only here we have the added advantage of frequent and predictable sunshine. Our first lesson was the difference between a *fiesta* and a *feria. Fiestas* or festivals are usually religious by nature and happen around feast days in the church calendar. These days in England we celebrate Christmas and Easter, although I fear that an increasing section of the population would be hard pressed to explain the relevance of either. In Spain it is still normal to shut up shop and mark the feast days of patronal saints, whether they be patron of the local church, of the province, region or country – or even, in some cases, patron saint of a business or factory. It is quite normal for a businessman to name his enterprise after a saint. Having done so it would be quite improper to carry on trading on the very day when that saint should be celebrated.

There are major festivals to mark the Epiphany, the coming of the three wise men to the nativity stable in Bethlehem. We know it in our secular society as Twelfth Night and over here it is referred to as the three kings festival or *Fiesta des Tres Reys*. For many Spaniards, especially builders it seems, *Tres Reys* marks the end of Christmas and there seems little point in bothering to get the laboring gear out for the odd day between these celebrations. This means that it is almost impossible to get any serious work done during this couple of weeks. *Tres Reys* is the time for present giving. And as always in Spain it is the children who come first, so this festival is predominantly a family affair where the youngsters are the centre of attention.

Children are always included in celebration here. Things are planned in a way that ensures that they are involved and take a full part in every party. We have been impressed at the way children are chaperoned. Grandmas or older brothers and sisters will protect the younger and more vulnerable members of the family, but in a way that lets them explore and partake. They are not held so tight that they cannot escape and are not placed in hygiene defensive playpens where they and danger may never meet. We have both jumped to save a toddler from tumbling into a swimming pool or steadying itself on the side of a red hot wood burning stove, but always the guiding hand of a senior relative has prevented disaster just at the crucial moment. Then, rather than admonish the infant, grandma or brother will explain how hot the stove is and demonstrate by holding the child close enough to feel the heat. The result is children who are wise to

danger and live a full life enjoying the whole of their environment.
At parties as elsewhere the Spanish treat their children with a marked respect. I will never forget the pain of visiting English pubs in the days when our sons were toddlers. Not only were we usually exiled to a cold drab room at the back; the worst thing of all was that they always seemed to serve the adults first. Presumably this was on the "children need to know their place" principle. Spanish families plan things around and for their children. Restaurant staff welcome children with a genuine enthusiasm. Children eat at the same time as their parents, from the same menu and in the same place. No Spaniard would ever dream of directing a family to a separate family room, unless it was for the real benefit of the children. And no Spanish child would be made to wait for food while parents were being served.
At Easter things close again to make way for the *Semana Santa* celebrations. Holy Week is still respected here, not as an excuse to visit the local garden centre to lay the summer bedding plants as seems to be the case in most of the UK. Here families work together to help prepare for the week of processions. The big processions are on the Wednesday, Thursday and Friday. First of course comes the children's procession on Wednesday, when all the smaller members of the family have their chance to carry specially scaled down religious statues in procession around the square. The youth bands from all around play and hundreds of children are lovingly dressed by proud parents to take their part.
Maundy Thursday sees the big evening procession. More than a dozen massive statues are brought out of the Church in town, to where they were previously delivered by the various village churches that form part of the parish. Each congregation takes pride in dressing its own float with flowers, and the men dress in heavy uniforms to carry the icon from their church. The floats are heavy. It takes 30 men or more to shoulder each in procession around the town. Bands play various forms of music and families form welcoming parties along the length of the route. This year the first float was brought out of the Church at just after 6pm. By 9 o'clock when we went to eat the procession was still moving slowly through the streets.
Diego, one of the local estate agents who had shown us properties was amongst the penitents carrying one of these massive statues. As he saw me he to me to tell me that next year it would be my turn to pay penance with pride. I'm really not sure that I would have the stamina, even if he had been serious. But I suppose that my "get out of jail free" card is my

faith – I am an Anglican and would almost certainly not be allowed to carry an icon of the Catholic Church.
On Good Friday morning a further procession through the part of town across the rambla stops the traffic and attracts almost equal volumes of spectators. No one would dream of popping off to do the weekly shop – even if any shops were open. They would not even consider viewing the procession and then going about their daily duties. Over here people take religious festivals seriously – so much so that Spain has one of the highest number of religious public holidays in Europe. I was surprised to be told that Germany is up there amongst the most celebratory. I don't picture them being swept by tradition or religious fervor. Somehow Germans always seem far too pragmatic to spend a day celebrating in this way. In Germany though I gather these occasions are used more for partying than for faithful devotion. In Spain they seem able to do both.
Spain celebrates saints' days, the Assumption, the Immaculate Conception and countless others. But in addition the Spanish are pretty good at partying for non-religious occasions. The *feria* or fair is a concept almost lost in England. Today fairs tend to be visiting funfairs, or perhaps a village carnival. But these have forgotten their origins in annual pagan or agricultural celebrations. Our first experience was the Albox *Feria del Almacien*. This food fair is where we first found the local olive oil, and were introduced to new cheeses, cured hams, wine and other goodies. But this commercial event was nothing compared to the village *ferias* that are the centre of village life. Towns have their own of course. In Albox the event runs over a weekend at the end of October and the area normally filled with clothing and household goods on market days is taken over instead by food and drink stalls. Every bar and hostal takes part, showing off its "house specialty". There are paella stands, the finest *jamon*, fresh soups and some of the best cheeses, including my favourite *queso curado*. Another legacy of Franco's fear of foreign trade is that French cheeses are known around the world, and British cheeses have a well-deserved reputation, while outside the Iberian Peninsular you are unlikely to find many people who have even heard of *Manchego*, the cheddar like variety, let alone the super blue veined cheeses and the dry, almost Parmesan dry hard cheese.
In our village the *fiesta* takes place in the middle of August. It therefore has the benefit of guaranteed good weather, and the consequent disadvantage of baking hot temperatures in this arid dry climate. Most of what happens here is laid on by the people

of the village themselves. The bars run stalls in the village squares, but it is the farmers and their wives who lay on the food. Makeshift barbecues burn long into the night, and local wine is in freely available. Pigs are roasted and the very best home cured hams are served. The village bakers lay on fine loaves, each large enough to feed several families.

The irony in all this is that in most rural communities the people of the land celebrate the harvest and express their thanks only once it is safely gathered in. Not so here. The almond harvest starts just after the village fair. You note that I carefully avoid saying "immediately" afterwards

But somehow activity must be possible during the weekend, probably induced by that same wine. This seems evident from the number of village people, both young and old who celebrate May birthdays. I have this picture of inebriated husbands almost falling upon their adoring wives, and sleeping off the effects for days after. The outcome of course must then be baptized. Only a few years later they will attend their first communion. Weddings follow and so the cycle goes on. These events often include a somber procession to the sanctuary and a very solemn blessing there. And at every event a full-scale celebration will be arranged, to ensure a day that no one will forget. The only problem is that members of the family will drink even more wine and other alcoholic refreshments that an unforgettable day can soon be forgotten.

Such is the nature of *fiestas* and *ferias* in Spain.

21 - Settling in

La Higuera had character, far more than any of the modern houses that we had previously owned, and the character was acquired over time, and through the changes of many generations.
However we have changed the house so much we have inevitably lost some of the features, but we have retained much of the character and added more. The old aluminum front door has gone, but in its place there now hangs a traditional hand made solid wood farmhouse door. The windows are also of a traditional build, with integral wooden shutters. But the real coup was the transformation of those roof beams. Now that we had opened the house up so much the ceilings stood out, and before Pedro got going on them they looked dull and dirty.
He and the project manager consulted on the best way to make a feature of the roof, and hit on a contrast feature. The untouched parts of the house have a wattle and daub style construction between the beams with pantiles hung over them. In the areas that had to be repaired a roof brick had been used. These lightweight hollow structure bricks are substantial and tough and with the help of concrete make a firm, secure and weatherproof roof. So Pedro created a smooth effect between the beams with a plaster finish, which is now painted in white. This left the problem of what to do with all those different styles of beam, old and new timber, concrete and tree trunks. Here came the clever solution. Firstly he filled in the concrete beams giving a rough edged effect, which created the same profile as the newer sawn timber beams. Then he applied a form of wood preservative, which has given these beams a uniform deep brown sheen.
This has given us a wonderful feature that draws the eye of everyone who visits the house. It did, though, use an amazing quantity of the treatment. Pedro quoted a fixed price for the decorating work that he did, and I can only imagine that he had no idea just how much of that gooey liquid he would need. We watched as the old timbers soaked up the liquid and seemed to remain unchanged. It would take four or five coats and then suddenly the deep brown sheen would appear. These must now

be some of the best-preserved timbers in Spain. Andréas tells me that he has never seen anything like it – but, like everyone else, he admires the result.

He's not so sure about some of the other things we've done though. The original windows were typically small. Some were as small as 10 inches by 12. The replacements are around three feet square, or slightly smaller. The effect is to change a dingy interior into a bright and welcoming space. He admits that, but he is slightly worried that we keep opening the shutters – "Too much sunlight is not good for the house". Now tell me how can a house suffer from too much sunlight?

Diego pointed out that the local opinion is that the inside of a home should be a haven on cool and peace, away from the harsh sun. There is some logic here. In daytime, unless the weather is bad, our neighbors are outside. They work outside and they relax outside, and although they may not watch their televisions outside like some Spanish townsfolk, they certainly take coffee outside. The insides of their houses are reserved for sleeping, both siesta and at night, and for avoiding the dark and the cold, when winter comes.

As a result their living space tends to be fairly restricted, and, like the French, they often live around the dining table. I remember being told many years ago that an hour spent at the dining table does not take you an hour closer to death. The latins believe that good food, good drink and good company are a way of borrowing time, and they still have regular family meals together in a way that is sadly dying out in Britain. I have not yet got my mind fully around the business of siesta. I have been convinced for years that my whole system is in severe decline at around 3pm. In attempts to avoid this I tend to eat very light lunches and Kathy and I usually eat our main meal in the evening. Yet every dietician seems to say that this is the worst way to treat our dietary tract – and the surest way to gain weight. I am living proof of the latter point. On the rare occasions that I do eat a full lunch I start to flag fast. My energy level drops and my thought processes suffer. Our son Mark explains that the blood flow is diverted to the alimentary system, depriving the brain of some of the oxygen it needs to function at full power. This seems to describe my situation perfectly – but how on earth does he come to know this? Perhaps hours sitting grazing in front of the TV are not so wasted after all.

Our Spanish neighbors all practice siesta and would be amazed if they knew that we do not always follow suit. Because of their fear of sunshine leaking into their homes the shutters are usually closed anyway, so it is not always easy to tell whether they are resting or not. But come three or four o'clock the telltale signs start to appear. The first is the lack of activity. The women doing their washing alongside the irrigation channels will have packed up. The goatherd and his flock will have settled down to rest, and any workmen will have laid down their tools. Tractors are silenced, and braying donkeys go quiet. Even the traffic flow reduces to almost nothing.

But there is a sign that we are still trying to decipher. Andréas and his wife Maria have a large old farmhouse that is really rather grand. The double front doors are high and wide and beautifully carved. Like most farm doors around here they have a door within a door construction, where an upper portion opens independently of the main door to allow fresh air - and occasionally even sunlight into the home. Some of these doors have an opening panel roughly two feet square in the top corner; ours have a similar sized opening in the centre of the upper part of the door. Andréas and Maria's front doors have a panel at the top of the left hand door that seems to be used as some sort of coded communication system.

Sometimes the doors and the panel are all securely shut, and we presume that this is a clear indication that they are not in or do not wish to be disturbed. Sometimes the left-hand door is flung wide, which would seem to be a welcoming gesture. But we are still trying to work out the meaning of the other three combinations, because these all rely on use of the flap. Sometimes the two doors are shut, but the flap is left wide open. Sometimes with the flap open a tea towel is draped over the door hanging through that flap - and sometimes the tea towel is there, but the flap is firmly shut. His brother, Pedro, simply explains that it is an important code. This is all the more intriguing. It seems to me that Andréas got to the "Do not disturb" sign principle long before any major hotel chain. Somehow he has managed to create a far more complex method of messaging than the "Do not disturb" and "Please make up my room" options that are the standard of hotels the world over.

One day in August while Andréas was showing me how the water system works (and I was running a few chapters behind him) he pointed to an overgrown weed around the tank. He explained that this weed was valuable because of the tiny fruit that it produced, as these could be pickled and very highly prized. I made note of this and tried hard to work out just what it was that he was talking about. All I could see was a mass of leaves.

This was just a few days before we returned to England and I thought no more about it.
It was around a fortnight later that I had a blinding revelation. I was talking with the project manager and he reported progress with the new terrace that Pepé was building for us. Kathy had identified that this end of the property would provide a fairly easy location for a large patio, and the most fabulous views out across the Sierra de los Filabres. We had agreed that he would arrange a six foot pavement along the rear of the house and carry on the tiles to create a wide terrace along the end, including paving over the concrete water tank. He had carefully planned the work to ensure that Andréas would be able to gain access to the tank, and assured me that his people would keep the tank locked to avoid any concern for Andréas.
On this call he explained that to keep the new tiling level we would need to add some steps, including five steps down from the main terrace, where we planned to put a table and chairs, to the top of the water tank where we planned to put sun loungers. He also discussed a retaining wall to hold the whole thing secure, and explained that the workmen had cleared away all the various vegetation. My vision cleared instantly as, too late, Kathy realized that what Andréas had shown me was a caper plant. That had now disappeared into a skip along with all the other weeds. What on earth would I say to Andréas? I needn't have worried – he had far bigger things to talk about when next we met.
Actually he had several contributions to make, but one of them was big – far bigger than I had imagined. I had expected the retaining wall, which I had agreed, to be capable of stopping the flowerbeds alongside our new patio from washing away. It will do that for sure. The wall is around 80 feet long. It runs along the side of the terrace and curves around the corner to run along the front of the old walled patio. The top sits at ground level alongside the terrace, and provides wide flowerbeds all around. But in places it is over 7 feet high. It has drainage holes to prevent water logging – and my mother in law has nicknamed it "The Great Wall of China". It is big, but as the builders explained it will provide the strength needed not only to retain the new pavement. It will also enable us to excavate my *cueva* and to build the planned new master bedroom on top without the need for expensive under-pinning.
Andréas cornered me when next we arrived and said he wanted to talk about the new wall. I could understand it. This structure was big. Well actually it was very big, and, to say the least, it

was a bit of a surprise. But in some ways Andréas' reaction was a bigger surprise. I was expecting a dressing down for allowing them to build such an overpowering structure, or words of wisdom on its design. But no. My *hombré* wanted to remark on what a good job Pepé and co. had made of this structure and how solidly it was constructed. He did have a suggestion, which was to continue the wall for a further few feet so that it blended into the "rockery" at the front of the house.
Otherwise he was very happy with it. It added substance and solidity I was told, and when told that it would be painted white to match the rest of the house my neighbor was delighted. I inquired about extending the wall as Andréas proposed, and was told that this should be left until after the new building was done one day. We now have to consider some form of bullustrading to stop visitors, especially the young and the old, from tumbling over the edge.
Andréas was very happy with all this. He told me once again that this wonderful new wall of ours is a feature, which has the added benefit that it will stop the terrace, and later the new bedroom, from settling in where they should not do so.

22 - Vivan las Diferencias

As we first drove towards town Kathy and I were surprised by the differences in scenery. But that surprise was nothing to the amazement that we felt when we first drove to Baza. This town sits on the main route from Granada to the East coast. Baza is a regional market centre. It has one of the largest street markets in the area – and Spanish markets are impressive at the best of times. But much more significantly it is the central livestock market for the eastern part of Andalucía and for parts of Murcia. As a result it is an important focus for the farming communities for hundreds of miles around.

Baza is high in the Sierras and from here it is an easy drive onwards to Granada and the ski slopes of the Sierra Nevada. As a result it is quite exposed and when the snows arrive or the cold winds blow it is Baza that they hit. When the TV weatherman, talks about snow in Almería be aware that Baza will be very cold. By contrast it might still be bright sunshine and very warm further down in the valleys.

From our house we have two options to reach Baza, both take around 40 minutes, and both are impressive drives. Over the Estancias past the Saliente is the mountain way. It meets the motorway at the old staging town of Chirivel, which has become almost a backwater since the opening of the motorway, as it bypasses the town. The other option is to take the main road from Albox – the one that has replaced the old railway line. This is an equally spectacular run, passing through hills and valleys and over grazing pastures. The contrast between these two journeys is quite surprising, and highlights a number of other local contrasts.

The colors here are all so much more intense than those that we see at home. The white snow and green trees on the sierras are part of this, but the deep colors of the various soils are perhaps the most concentrated. On the Albox to Baza road we pass through areas of rich red almost African soils, where sunset seems to mirror the colors of the fields. But even here the small field cultivation style of many hundreds of years and the geological strata have created a patchwork of colors, deep reds, and rich browns with shades of mahogany and chestnut. These rich colors create a sense of warmth on even the coldest of days. The mountain drive over the Estancias presents a very different view. Here we pass by fields of slate gray soil. As the sun reflects off these areas it creates an impression of lakes of water on a cold day. Even on the same winter day and at the same temperature the lower road can make one feel warm, while the mountain route will induce the shivers. In summer the same effects can have a reverse comfort effect, as the rich reds and browns will serve to increase the effect of the sun and leave one feeling quite stifled in the heat. At the same time the slate gray fields near the Saliente can create a subconscious cooling.

On that first drive to Baza, in December, we headed north towards Chirivel and joined the motorway there. As we came closer to Baza we could see the snow-capped peaks around Sol y Nieva and the rich greens of the lower slopes. We hit Baza at siesta time – we are quite good at doing that sort of thing. So we drove round the town and headed back towards home along the main road. At this point we were still finding our way – and we still had not found either Hiper Amica or the olive press co-operative! But the drive back towards Huercal Overa was stunning. I had to keep stopping by the side of the road to walk out and appreciate those views. I pointed my little camera in every direction and just kept snapping. The air was crisp and fresh, and the snow on the mountaintops was stimulating, but the rich soils reflected the sunshine and we stood there without coats convinced in our subconscious that we were warm.

The differences in soil are at their extreme alongside the *autovia* just near to Lorca. A cutting leads into two tunnels – one in each direction – and the cutting itself has scored into the hills to the west of the town. The impressive bit is a multi-colored cliff face that bears ten or twelve shades of earth, and reminds Kathy of the cliffs at Alum Chine. As a child she visited the Isle of Wight with her family and remembers vividly the multi-colored sands for which the bay is famous. She was anxious to take our boys there when they were young and we still have small bottles carefully filled by them with different colored layers of this naturally rainbow tinted sand. No doubt one day some enterprising Spaniard will set up a similar business selling the soil near Lorca.

Kathy had commented on our first visit how the produce reflected the environment. I knew about the rich plains of Spain – after all I've seen My Fair Lady! So it was always clear to me that once one leaves the hot Mediterranean coastline and heads over the coastal sierras one gradually moves into the fertile arable lands of inner Spain. Neither of us though had appreciated just how much the farming and its produce could change in just 20 or so miles. Along the narrow coastal plain of Almería sit these plastic covered hothouses, where some of Europe's best fruit, salads and flowers are produced.

The technique is known as *plasticultura*, and nearly 40,000 acres of the coastal area are covered in these plastic greenhouses. The effect is the illusion that they merge into the sea as the sun is reflected off both the water and the plastic. This was once very fertile terrain, but after the Moors departed the quality of the farming deteriorated and up to the 1950s the area was barren. A new cultivation method, known as the sand plot technique was introduced. This involves a layer of packed in clay, which prevents water loss into the soil below, a layer of well-rotted manure (which is replaced every few years) and finally a layer of clean sand from the beach, which prevents evaporation. The first greenhouse appeared over one of these sand plots in the early 60s, but it was in the next decade that they suddenly seemed to multiply. Around 80 to 100 feet long these plastic tunnels are carefully maintained in a suitably humid micro-climate by a trickle watering process, which these days is controlled by computers. The *alhondigs*, or co-operatives, which market the produce, are now selling throughout northern Europe and even airfreighting salad stuff to the USA.

Just behind these naturally arid areas, which have been converted by man, irrigation and plastic into highly productive mass market gardens, sit the citrus groves of this area. The drive from the coastal motorway towards Albox passes from the polythene towers, through deep green fields in the bases of the valley and past fields of orange and lemon trees. These trees usually fruit twice each year, depending on the variety and the local climate. Here three crops are not unusual, so it is quite normal to see fruit on the trees, and at times the powerful scent of the blossom permeates the air. Orange blossom is one of those wonderful reminiscent smells that can instantly bring back all sorts of happy memories. Why is it that scents have such an evocative effect? Kathy's senses still rise in an instant whenever she smells hibiscus as it reminds her of sultry tropical nights on a vacation in Jamaica over 20 years ago.

Further in on the journey towards Baza the terrain changes again and one passes the first of the uncultivated quarrying areas, where stone takes priority over crops, and then into the hill country around us. Here the fields are more open, and more exposed to the winds. These can create a wonderful cooling breeze in summer, but on the coldest of winter days they can also bring warmer air from the coast. The winds also have an erosive effect on the soil and mean than the potential for crops here is quite limited. Almonds and olives have become established largely because neither requires irrigation. Once the trees have made themselves at home they need little more than a plough once or twice a year, an occasional pruning and then comes the backbreaking task of harvest. There are said to be some 250 million olive trees in Spain, and 80% of the countries gargantuan production of olive oil comes from the region of Andalucía. Spain is one of the most prodigious producers of olive oil in the world - and even exports to Italy! I am proud that our few trees make their contribution.

And, of course, it's all so different to the landscape we are used to at home. We have lived in the Test Valley in Hampshire for around 12 years now and are used to the greens and yellows of the English countryside, enhanced in autumn by the shades of fall, and camouflaged in winter following the defoliation. The contrasts with Spain are enormous. It is not just the differences within Spain that are so emphatic. Later on in our first year we drove out on a chilly day and up through that same route towards Baza. I felt just the same sense of warmth. Yet here we were surrounded by snow-covered fields where the reddish browns were peaking through the thin covering of snow. The sun was reflected off both the snow and the soil, and I was delighted by the mixed sensations of chill and warmth that this created. By the time we reached Baza the snowfall was lying quite thickly. But in town the snow on the rooftops was starting to melt. It was market day and we emerged from our nice warm little car to find everyone walking around in snow boots and winter overcoats. We had left home on a chilly but sunny day, and were dressed in jumpers but had not come prepared for a winter sports environment. In fact, as so often, we had driven out with no plan of where we would go. So these obvious foreigners were wandering around a winter market surrounded by folk whose dress would be just as appropriate in the Christmas markets of Munich or Warsaw. They looked so different to the people who we had seen the day before on our own market.

In Baza the old ladies were wrapped up like Russian Babushkas and the men were dressed in coats scarves and thick woolen hats. Everyone up there wore boots and they carried their shopping in old and well-used baskets. Many of the market

traders had gas heaters burning and there were huddles of shivering shoppers knocking back *carajillo* with their *churos*.
Churos is a staple of every market and every fair all over Spain. It is a form of long, thin, crisp and usually fresh doughnut. The dough is fed into a large circular vat of oil, heated over an over-sized open butane gas ring. The stallholder forces the mixture through a large nozzle like the type my mother used to use for icing cakes. This gives the end result a six-pointed cross-section, creating a large surface area for the oil to fry to a crisp outer covering. The mixture is spiraled into the oil, thus the end result is a deep fried dough, coiled to resemble a garden hose. The frying takes just a few moments at a very high temperature, thus guaranteeing a crisp outside and a doughnut consistency inside. Once cooked it is chopped with kitchen shears into curved lengths of around eight inches, and covered in sugar applied from a shaker.
Carajillo is an extra warming coffee. It is a *café solo*, an espresso, as many people would call it. Traditionally it is finished off with a flaming brandy. Today though most bars simply add a tot of *coñac* to the plain black coffee, and in my experience it has just the right effect on a chilly day. I do have to restrain myself when I'm driving though, so in Baza I just settled for a double *café solo.*
In the local market a few days before most people were still wearing just shirts and jumpers or lightweight anoraks, and they were standing outside the various bars drinking beer. As always the *cerveza* was served so cold that the glasses were covered in condensation, which marks the chilled temperature of the contents. The sun was shining in both towns, just a short drive apart, but the temperature and hence the whole atmosphere was completely different.
Talking of differences I am always amused, and often frustrated by the latin nationals lack of awareness of their own body space and the special needs of others. We British are often too reserved and sometimes too respectful of others – I acknowledge this. But in southern countries it seems that attitudes can go a little too far the other way. Take for example the business of queuing. Or perhaps I should say the lack there of. In Britain we queue almost religiously and jump the queue only at our peril. The wrath of a Lancashire housewife or a Wiltshire farmer's wife is simply not worth bearing in exchange for jumping two places nearer the front.
In Spain though everything is based around the total absence of a queue. If you see chaos in their apparent lack of system stand

back one day and observe. You will doubtless see that customers are served in almost direct order of their arrival. How the shopkeeper or stallholder knows I cannot tell – especially as they always seem oblivious to arrivals and departures amongst the throng around the counter. But somehow they do. All the jostling is no more than posturing and a simple lack of awareness of others. It implies no disrespect and is in no way related to stress or tension. Indeed these apparently hyperactive shoppers are in truth far more relaxed in their labors than their up-tight English counterparts. We are so worried about not letting a little old lady jump the line that we miss the point that she has only one tin of beans to buy and is probably a darned sight more weary than the rest of the shoppers. In the post office a new arrival will ask who is the *ultimo* or last and hence the person that this new person will follow. It works!

The more difficult aspect to which to accustom one's self though is the lack of spatial awareness. Families will just stop in the midst of a surging throng of shoppers to chat with one another about plans for the weekend or grandma's current medical condition. They are not being rude when they block your way. They are just completely unaware that they are doing so. They are the most caring people you could imagine, and would be gravely hurt if they thought that we might be in the least stressed by their apparent lack of awareness. So the problem is clearly ours for ever allowing ourselves to become worked up by the local residents who are simply going about their lives as they and their forbears have done for centuries.

Why on earth would it matter that someone stops suddenly, thus providing a perfect static weapon on which to crush one's face? They don't get worked up by it, and many of what have become known as the ill behaved tourists from northern Europe are simply reacting as they were trained to the Spaniards behaving as they were brought up. Observe the arguments and rudeness of mixed crowds in a tourist town. Often they result from a local or group of locals socializing in the way of tourists, or failing to stand in an orderly line at a shop counter. Why should they – they were not trained to do so, and the system works just fine this way? But the visitors are used to a very different culture and cannot get used to the idea that this behavior is not a manifestation of Mediterranean bad manners. Because the Spanish are actually very well mannered – it just happens that their manners are different to ours.

And so it should continue. The magic of this wonderful place would be lost immediately if life were as predictable as life at home and we all shared a common behavior. It is these very differences that help to create the enchantment of life in the hills of Almería. We are so lucky and long may these differences last.

23 - The other side of the Euro

I have said very clearly why we wanted to live in the country. Rural Spain has excited us and enthralled us, and our decision to live in the hills has been richly rewarded day after day. However I know very well that this is not everyone's cup of sangria. Kathy's parents were the first resident adventurers in the family and bought their first property in the early 80s. They chose a cozy apartment with a wonderful sun terrace on the edge of the old fishing town of Torrevieja in Alicante province. The objective was to create a bolt hole, where they could both escape the hectic round of hard work that paid for it.
They bought a real bargain at a time when owning a property in the sun was no more than dream for most working families. They had been dreaming for several years of a house in the sun and, with no intention of buying, they followed up one of those advertisements you see in the Sunday press. David and Edith are both pretty astute and also fairly cautious, so they were not about to jump into anything that might leave them in trouble. They had worked damned hard to create a reasonable financial cushion, and they had no intention of risking it on anything risky in Spain.
So they researched the subject very carefully, and as they were amongst the pioneers in terms of real people owning second homes abroad there was little published data to go on. At that time the whole process in Spain was even more risky than it is today, and the British government's decision to remove exchange controls certainly wasn't matched by the Spanish authorities. They wanted to know where every peseta came from, and as for pounds - you were expected to obtain notarized documents authorizing and confirming the import of foreign currency.
They told us about a bungalow development and said that they planned to go on an inspection flight to have a look around. My in-laws are not the type to be intimidated or rushed into a decision that did not suit their purpose. So we knew that if they were not entirely satisfied they would come home and explain

pragmatically that they had found nothing for them and wait until they did. Their weekend on the southern Costa Blanca introduced them to a new part of Spain away from the glitz of Benidorm and Torremolinos, but with the urban facilities that were a part of their normal life. They were well fêted while they were there, and met several other couples in just the same position.

They decided to invest around $13000 in this promise of a maisonette. What they actually bought was an artist's impression, the chalk marks on a plot of land and a dream. And in exchange for all that they left behind a deposit and brought home a very legal looking contract. The developer was a major national name and lived up to every promise. The apartment was completed as promised just four months later and for less than $4000 was well furnished. That little vacation home served our family well for nearly 10 years. We used it for countless vacations with the children, with friends and with my parents when they were alive. We visited for weekends and extra breaks and became quite used to the idea of several vacations a year where one or two of these trips would be spent in *La Casita Blanca.*

Edith and David have said many times that the pleasure that they derived from that place meant that it owed them nothing. Add our trips and family and friends and it would be impossible to achieve such good value, except perhaps in a tent. The other benefit is that we all became familiar with the Spanish way of life and gained a new and growing international cadre of friends. The town has continued to grow and is now a small city by the sea. The major attractions driving this growth have been the proximity to countless good beaches, the fact that Torrevieja is still a Spanish town, with many working residents, the closeness of Alicante Airport, and the United Nations research proving that this corner of Spain is one of the healthiest places in Europe.

Alicante has several flights a day from various UK airports, ranging from package vacation charter flights with amazingly low seat only prices, to full scale scheduled services from all four London airports. It has all the usual services of an international airport, including car hire at prices per week that would not look out of place as daily prices in northern Europe. Torrevieja is around half an hour away by motorway, and is not under any of the usual flight paths, so it has all the benefits and none of the disadvantages

The fact that this is still a real Spanish place is demonstrated by the fact that on certain beaches it is still quite common to find

Spanish families doing pretty much what they have always done. Grandma will sit under a beach umbrella in her head to toe black outfit. She will look after the young children and allow them just enough freedom to enjoy themselves, without ever being more than a quick grab away in case of the slightest whiff of danger. The parents will promenade up and down the beach hand in hand, looking beautiful and so much in love. The older children will play in the sea, again always in sight of grandma, and the young adults will play volleyball in everyone else's way. When lunchtime comes an enormous collection of cool boxes and hampers will appear and a wonderful spread party will be laid out. They then go home just as the English appear – "Mad dogs …"

One thing that will not – ever – appear on these "Spanish" beaches is a bare breast. Topless bathing is now tacitly allowed all over Spain, but there are some places where it simply does not happen. Convention dictates that in certain places the visitor should respect the sensitivities of the locals, and fortunately it is still so. So although Torrevieja is now a busy town, where traffic and parking can be murder in August, it is still quite definitely a Spanish town. The resident population is a real mix of nationalities and cultures, with Swedes, Czechs, Dutch, Austrians, Brits – the lot.

David and Edith became increasingly familiar with the area, and felt more and more at home there. They both worked every hour they could at home in Cheshire and as a result their leisure time tended to be agglomerated, and turned into time together in Spain. This meant that a whole new social life was created, around a new set of friends. Add to that the challenge of feeling good in the middle of what would be a dank wet day in England, compared to the joys of clear skies and bright days – even in the middle of winter – and you start to see why their lives drifted towards the Costa Blanca.

As they became more established so they gained new and varied friends. Remember that the locals here come from all over Europe, and with their very cosmopolitan outlook they settled in very well. So much so that by 1990 they tended to see Torrevieja as home and Greater Manchester as the place they had to keep going back to earn enough to pay for it all. When David was offered an early retirement package a year or so after Edith retired from the Civil Service he had to contain his reflex reaction, which was probably to kiss his boss and jump for joy. After all he was being told that he was on the scrap heap. His valuable skills as a trained and very experienced engineer,

gained over decades of hard work, were no longer required. And he was expected to be mortally wounded. Somehow he managed to cope without the need for counseling, and whooped for joy as soon as he was out of earshot of the boss.
And it helped them make one decision, and not many months later they initiated the process to sell up and move out to the sun. They did it all in a very measured way and eventually moved around 18 months later. At first they lived in their little maisonette until they could find the house that they wanted to move to. And from there they moved into a beautiful classic white villa with pool in a quiet residential street. They have shops and bars a reasonable walk away, plus a pharmacy and doctor's surgery, church, restaurant and anything else you might need to make a new life. La Siesta is a very pleasant all residential area. It has a number of houses that are owned by non-residents who still have to toil in their various countries of origin. But it has none of the frenetic style of a big seaside resort; none of the hassles of living in a place over-run by tourists. Many visitors come and go, but there they tend to be property owners themselves, or their families and friends.
So they live in an urban area very different to our village home. They also live a rather different life style to us. Firstly let me use Edith's analogy to deal with the "what do you find to do all day?" question. People who retire to warmer climates are regularly asked this question as if it must be a soulless and boring experience. As she points out she does just the same things here that she would have done if she were still living in England. She does the shopping. She does the housework. She cooks and washs up. And so on. The difference of course is that when she has finished her chores she is rarely confined to the house by bad weather outside. On most days of the year one can sit in the sun or the shade and get the benefit of the clear skies and the higher light values. I am absolutely convinced of the correctness of the experts who talk about "SAD" syndrome. The lack of light in a northern European winter has a direct effect on my mood - and on most of the people around me.
The other big difference is that brighter skies and warmer nights encourage people to venture out more often. We live a rather quiet life down here, but just a couple of hours up the motorway my in-laws and their friends face a constant test of their stamina. While we will have a drink in the village bar, or dinner with friends, the crowd in Torrevieja have an endless string of social events and a real problem fitting it all in, without causing offence to someone. I remember a few years ago when they

would still come home for a month or so a couple of times a year. We would have a job keeping up with them as they dashed about fitting in shopping, visits to friends, hairdressers, dressmakers, opticians, dentists and so on. Indeed Kathy would point to their arrival, use of the washing machine and hectic itinerary and talk about her delinquent parents. It was almost like having two extra teenagers in the house - except that they were tidy - and polite!

Today, although David is sadly no longer with us, Edith still has as much energy - and far more than we can muster after a busy working week. She runs a monthly dinner dance for one local club, and they help with charity raffles through another. She pop off on *pensionistas* outings, which are great value thanks to local government subsidy. And I still have a job keeping up with what she is up. Whenever one of their friends has family over the whole crowd are brought together like a clan re-union to welcome the return of a prodigal son or daughter.

They have barbecues, pool parties, cocktails, lunches on the beach and suppers by moonlight. They don't ever seem to need an excuse for a celebration, and with such a large circle of friends there seems to be a birthday celebration almost every week.

The other question people ask is "What happens if you are ill?" The answer is simple. The social health service in Spain is amongst the best in the world and the UK has a reciprocal health service arrangement with Spain, as part of the European Community. As a result any registered British citizen is entitled to free medical treatment at the level provided to Spanish residents. This includes free prescriptions for the "Third Age" citizens, children etc. It also provides excellent emergency clinic treatment and very good quality hospital treatment, often with much shorter waiting times than at home. There is a difference though. Nursing care tends to be restricted to medical nursing, changing of dressings, observations, monitoring of drips and medication etc. The nurses duties do not usually include bathing, or even feeding. So here the family and friends have an important role to play. And it has a wonderful effect of bringing the patient closer to his loved ones. Here as in most places private medical insurance will speed things up, and is one luxury chosen by many.

The other important role for friends is the same sort of job that neighbors undertake anywhere else. Often wives of patients are reliant on their friends for lifts to and fro, or help with the shopping. Informal self-help groups are an important part of society here just as they are anywhere else. The difference between our life and theirs though is that they get a lift from an English-speaking friend of a similar age in a familiar looking saloon car. We will happily accept a lift organized by one Spanish neighbor, but provided by another we have not previously met – and possibly in a trailer towed behind a motorized cultivator.

David and Edith and their friends have a high life and a healthy life. And the one of the similarities between theirs and ours is one of the essential differences between life out here and life at home – the cost of living. Whichever side of the euro you choose you need a lot less of them to have a good standard of living and a good life-style out here.

24 - Lazy Days

Spain is known for two types of climate. That My Fair Lady song "The rain in Spain falls mainly on the plane" might leave the understandable mis-conception that the Spanish interior is a miserable rainy place. And from years of package vacations and TV travel programs we all know that the Spanish *costas* are hot and sunny. After all no one remembers ever seeing the presenters in a raincoat.

As always the truth is not quite as black and white. It is true that most of Spain's rainfall occurs in land and away from the Mediterranean coast. The main dairy farming regions of Spain are in the north of the country and most of the arable farming occurs in the interior. It is also a fact though that these same areas share much of the warmth of the coasts and regularly beat the resort temperatures. One other factor ignored in these bland generalities is the relative humidity of various places. It took us some time to work out that the Costa Dorada, in southern Catalonia, is more uncomfortable than the Costa Blanca because of higher levels of ambient humidity. It also took my slow brain a while to realize that Teruel is more comfortable than its coastal neighbors, and the difference once again was to do with humidity. At my size clamminess can be an important factor in determining comfort, and so I tend to have a good idea of the dryness or dampness of local climates quite precisely.

So avoiding known high humidity areas seemed a good idea in choosing our future home and it was by chance rather than good planning that we discovered the remarkably low humidity of this part of Spain. For some it is unbearable, and to those I can only say, "try the Costa Dorada". But for us it is heaven. The southeastern portion of the Iberian Peninsular is renowned for its predominantly dry climate. The coastal strip of Almería is naturally more comfortable, making the resorts of Mojacar and Garrucha easy places in which to relax.

On the trip where we found that first house, *Cortijo Oliverico,* we had to do some weird planning to get back home, and as I have already said this included staying the night in a motel near Barcelona Airport. Our journeying took us from the dryness of the sierras to the slightly damper coastal climate and on up to Torrevieja, where we stayed the night with Kathy's family. As we stepped out of the hire car there I knew that even in the two-hour drive we had passed into a closer atmosphere, not severely uncomfortable, but distinctly different. From there we flew next day to Barcelona on an unimpressive domestic flight, and it was the dampness hanging in the air as the aircraft door was opened that brought home to us both the massive difference in moisture between these various places. As I now understand the northern costas are renowned for their relatively clammy atmosphere, and the location that we have chosen is one of the driest in Europe. For me that is just wonderful. We have all the water we need, and both drink several quarts a day, even in winter. That the water is so good is a real bonus.

The high temperatures and the shortage and irregularity of rainfall, and the torrential nature of what does fall, are the causes of the eroded landscape. They also lead to the poor vegetation and the low agricultural yields that have formed the style of farming in this area. The average annual rainfall is around 300 mm. In old money that means only twelve inches of rain each year. And if that were not enough almost all of it can fall at once, hence the *barrancas (flood river courses)*. On average it only rains on 40 days each year – and that includes minor showers. The worst rainfalls in recent history occurred in 1973, 6 inches fell in March, equivalent to 21% of that year's total. In October 1918 though 10 inches rainfall was recorded in just 48 hours.

The average annual temperature is 65^0, represented by a high of around 85^0 in August and the occasional January frost. But these things are not always as predictable as we might like. In 1955 the July high reached 81^0 and in February that same year a temperature of 90^0 was recorded – by contrast December 1970 saw a low of 24^0.

So it's not always predictable – but it has to be said that more often than not we wake to sunshine and on most days we can enjoy our breakfast or lunch outside. Now how often could you do that in England? The heat does incline one to laziness and I soon discovered where the "*mañana*" theory of Spanish idleness comes from. *Mañana* means both tomorrow and morning, but no one should assume that the Spanish who talk about doing something *mañana* are being lazy or work shy. There is a strong and hard working streak amongst Spanish laborers and, when well directed, our impression is that they work at least as well as

their British counterparts. The difference is in the way they do that work, and this takes some understanding.
An important difference though is in the priorities that we each set on various tasks, and the order of action. My impatience means that I want everything done now. Kathy, by contrast, leaves everything until it can wait no longer. So when we travel I annoy her by getting the suitcase out the weekend before we leave and starting the process of finding and sorting clothes. She by contrast, and to my annoyance, will leave everything until the evening before a six am departure to the airport. At 10 o'clock my wife is still putting things in the washing machine and furiously ironing, and twenty minutes before we leave she has been known to give up and stuff everything in the suitcase saying "I'll sort it out when we get there." Who is to say which of us is right?
The Spanish have what appears to be a thoroughly disorganized way of doing things. Yet somehow it works. Laborers will undertake finishing work before the main structure is in place, and trying to get things done differently is more likely to result in them stopping work rather than doing it "my way". I was surprised to walk into our house one day to see Pepé tiling the splash backs in the kitchen. I was not only surprised that he had reached this point in the job so soon. I was amazed to see the tiles going up while the walls were un-plastered and the floor un-laid. In England we have had various building work done over the years, from new build to restoration and conversion, and in all those jobs wall tiles have been about the last thing to be put in place.
I was even more surprised to see that all the wall tiles were in place in the main bathroom – before any of the sanitary fittings had been installed. OK the bath was there, but everywhere else was bare walls. No toilet, no basin etc. In fact – no floor. When I asked why I was told that of course the tiles had been fitted first. Why? Well they always do it this way. In fact the walls were plastered above the tiles quite late in the process, and the tiles themselves are fitted, and very skillfully, directly onto the concrete of the wall. They have a way of doing things you see.
Some time later, just before the painter was due to do his stuff; we discovered that in our careful planning we had managed to place one of the bedside light switches inconveniently behind the headboard. In fact we had assumed that the bed would be placed centrally along the wall and hence planned for the switches to be fitted a few inches on either side. Neither of us had allowed for the wardrobe which had to stand in the room, and which (of

course) had the effect of moving the bed off centre. As a result the switch on my side of the bed would be just and tantalizingly out of reach, while to turn off the light from her side of the bed Kathy would need to reach around behind the headboard. These contortions were bound to prove a challenge – and we decided that such challenges we could do without. So we asked Pepé to move both switches and their adjoining sockets the necessary short distance, and to do so before Pedro started to wield his paintbrush. No point in having to bring him back again to touch up the work, when it could all be properly planned – I thought.
But others had different ideas, and next time we saw the house our bedroom furniture had been delivered and the inside had been painted a wonderful clean and bright-glowing white. Obviously everything had been finished so we wandered round with pride. And there in the bedroom the new wardrobe, bed and drawers fitted in perfectly. We were really proud that we had chosen so well. Not only was the size right, but the style helped to protect the feel of the house. Everyone agrees that this has the feel of a traditional Spanish bedroom. And the light switches? Well no they were still where they had originally been placed. When I asked Pepé about them, in a calm but concerned way, he explained that they would be moved *"mañana"*. "But why didn't you move them before the painting was done and the furniture was delivered?" I asked. "It is better this way" was the standard response. And the next day? Well nothing happened actually, but just a few days later those power points were moved and shortly afterwards Pedro appeared to paint the fresh plaster. Today you wouldn't know that there had ever been any problem.
So the system works – in its own way. There is little point in trying to change the way things are done, partly because they know their way of doing things, and partly because of that stubborn streak that is the trait of all latin people, which does not allow them to take advice from others – even those who are paying the bill.
Being rather inept at DIY allows me to enjoy other aspects of life here, and lazing in the sun falls into that category. On our first summer stay in the house we spent nearly ten days rushing around getting things done. I did my fair share of putting up and fixing and really managed rather well. But we also got to know the town swimming pool, where we had first met the film crew. Not many towns can boast such a large and such a well-kept pool. Obviously some mayor or other decided that he was going to "give" the town a legacy that would ensure his popularity for years to come.

Under Latin Skies

Just above the *rambla* run these two paved tracks, one on either side, where traffic take a host of short cuts from one part of town to another, or out to the bypass. On the eastern side there is a small memorial park under the shadow of the high bridge and beyond that is a large park with tennis courts, sports pavilion and the municipal pool. It is massive and surrounded by well-maintained grass – the course Mediterranean variety. The surprise for us is not that everyone talks about how lucky they are to have this wonderful facility that all the children love, but that so few of them seem actually to use it. It is always quiet and when the locals use the pool they stay for an hour and leave. It seems to be a stopping off point for busy shoppers to cool off their tiring children, but, unlike the foreigners, the locals don't seem to stay for a day. We haven't seen a Spanish cool box in our visits there. This could be partly because the restaurant attached to the pool is so good, but is more likely because the Spanish see this as a local convenience rather than an attraction for a day out.

Our village also has a public swimming pool. Remember that this is a small rural village. It has one church, two bars, a village shop and a swimming pool. How many British villages could boast such a facility I wonder? It is inevitably smaller than the pool in town, and it does not boast the same lush green setting. In fact it sits elevated alongside the road at the northern end of the village. It is surrounded by a paved area and high chain link fencing, and adjoins two hard surface tennis courts. But like its bigger sibling it is carefully supervised, and the children tend to gather in late afternoon to play and cool off together. For a place with such a super year round climate I still fail to understand why both these swimming pools are open for just two months a year. In both cases they open towards the end of the summer term for end of term galas and close two months later at the end of August. It seems such a waste, when, even without heating, the facilities could be in use from May to September without any difficulty.

But for a restless soul like me being lazy can take on very different faces. I thoroughly enjoy pottering around our fields doing things to the almond trees. I have no idea whether what I do contributes in any way to their well-being, but I am fairly sure that I do no harm. I certainly have yet to be chastised by Andréas, and I am sure that he would tell me if I were wrong! But I also find that the bright skies and peaceful environment, helped by the clean air, give me a greater sense of well-being. I can tackle a day's office work here in half the time, and as a result am far more productive in the work I do here than ever anyone can be in an office. We are also far better housekeepers here. The fact that almost every morning we can throw open the windows and welcome in the sun, not only shows up the dust so much more clearly – it also gives one a fresh motivation to tackle the very same jobs that have been done day in day out – and will need to be done day in and day out in the future, with just as much enthusiasm.

In the summer evenings here we laze in the light of the setting sun, often with a glass of very ordinary red wine, and in winter we cozy up in the warmth of the wood burning stove. There is no inclination to shut ones self away from the privations of winter, because we know that if it rains tomorrow the sun will almost certainly shine the following day. Somehow being lazy takes on a whole new meaning here.

25 - Never on a Sunday

Until you really get into the swing of things fiestas seem to jump up and grab you when you least expect them. It seems to me that the measly British count of 8 public holidays a year is by far the lowest in Europe. I deal with many nationalities and I am constantly finding them shut for one festival or another. Most tend to be religious, followed closely by various national or community days. Large parts of Belgium shut in celebration of the French speaking community, and on an unrelated occasion some of the same outlets close along with others to celebrate the Flemish speaking community. The 17th November is the day of Prayer and Repentance in Germany, and Spain celebrates Constitution Day on 6th December, followed by large tranches of Europe shut for the feast of the Immaculate Conception – or the "Immaculate Contraception" as one business answer phone message put it. At least they had tried to provide information to their English-speaking callers.
In Belgium businesses tend to shut and staff seem to spend the day catching up on sleep or visiting the local DIY store. In Spain these days are respected almost universally with every store closed for the day. This might not be so bad were it not for the fact that so many of these celebrations fall on a Monday, and in the less developed parts of Spanish society it is still traditional for everything to shut on a Sunday. Now once you get used to all this it is easy to enjoy the peace of the regular long weekend when you simply cannot shop. It is also rather good for the wallet. And it is only a few years since public holidays in Britain also meant that everything was closed. As a child a bank holiday Monday meant that everywhere would be shut from close of business on Saturday until Tuesday morning. And in the case of the banks and offices from close of business on the Friday.
Today though we have become used to a far more convenience based society, where even the village shop is open until 7pm or later most evenings and at least until lunch-time on Sundays. Public holidays have been re-defined as a day when those who work probably receive time and a half, while those who don't buy from those who do. The garden centers record their highest sales

of the year on Good Friday, Easter Monday and the May public holidays. In the big Spanish cities it is not impossible to find shops open on holidays, and the larger hypermarkets and other warehouse stores on the outskirts may well be open on Sundays. In high season in the cosmopolitan resorts it is difficult to notice the difference between a Sunday or a feast day and normal day. The only clue is probably that the bank is closed and the church is open – but with automatic teller machines you might have to search hard to see even that sign.

Here things are different. We have tended to fly from the UK on Saturdays. It is a convenient use of official annual leave and allows Kathy to do her last minute washing and packing in a more relaxed atmosphere. We quickly learned that shops are shut on a Sunday and accepted that fresh food would be impossible without a long drive to somewhere like Murcia. It took longer to work out that whatever my Financial Times diary might say about public holidays we should assume that everywhere would be shut on the Monday as well. Why should we assume this? Simply because experience had taught us this lesson.

The other difficult – even painful – lesson is that festivals and feast days vary by area. Not only do different regions celebrate different saints days. Different provinces and even towns shut down at different times. On one occasion we had a fruitless (literally) visit to a local market. We found only a handful of produce stalls where we had expected the usual busy street market offering clothes, linen, ironmongery etc. Kathy hankered after a big town. This was around 11am on a Monday, and the nearest big town to where we then were, was Lorca, around a 50-minute drive away. We headed there on the *autovia.* It didn't occur to us that Lorca might be closed; after all we had been walking in and out of shops all morning.

So it was that we drove in to Lorca at midday – alone. The town was well and truly shut and I felt much as I did on the day we visited Mini Hollywood. We visited the centre and saw all the signs of a ghost town. Every shop was shuttered and every bar was closed. There wasn't even a meal to be had – in fact even the fast food outlets had slowed down to a halt. We sought out the main church to establish just what festival we had been hit by – and it too was bolted. So we drove to the two edge-of-town hypermarkets, expecting that they at least would be open – perhaps just until lunchtime though. Mercadona was firmly closed with not a light on in the place, and Eroski at the *centro comercial* was equally securely shut.

As a result we hit two, and very different, reactions. Mine was to comment that this was our third visit to Lorca, and that we had yet to find it open. We called in one Monday en-route from the family to Albox. We drove through the town and didn't see one other human being on our way through. The second time had been on a Sunday – foolish, as we now know. We had been on our way to pick up Mark at an agreed hand-over point outside a BP gas station alongside the motorway. We had judged that this was roughly equidistant between Torrevieja and Albox and hence a fair split of driving between us and Edith and David. On that occasion Lorca was equally shut, but we did pass a church as the congregation was leaving. So we had established that life does (sometimes) exist in the town. Had it not been for that I would have been tempted to disbelieve everything else I had been told – convinced instead that Lorca was in truth a ghost town.

Our more discerning neighbors seem to do their big shopping in Lorca or Almería, which are roughly equidistant from us. They seem to find the stores they need without problem and, more to the point, seem to find it open! But not us.

Kathy's reaction to this latest wasted journey was rather more troubled than mine. She had wanted to wander around a big market, or failing that a big store – withdrawal symptoms were taking over and she was suffering from a severe retail deprivation. She was very upset and I was at the receiving end of all that anguish. At the time we were using a rather underpowered little Hyundai car, which the day before had experienced some difficulty getting up our drive. By the time we left Lorca we had spent the best part of two hours in what to me at that point to be a useless little tin box, which should never have been given clearance to travel on the public highway.

We left Lorca in floods of emotion and I took two wrong turnings before finding my way back onto the motorway – one of those wrong turnings led us into a manure rich pig farm, which had the effect of giving the car a very fitting coating of the stuff by which I had come to describe this vehicle.

We drove back down the motorway in glorious November sunshine and to varying strains of car mis-firing, Kathy just firing, and me just missing. By the time we reached Puerto Lumbreras, the next main town I was feeling thoroughly victimized. I had a car that wanted to fail on me, and a wife who insisted on making me feel guilty about my own performance and that of the car. And the real irony was that although I now loathed that little car I found myself defending it against Kathy's onslaught.

One of the reasons for wanting to do some "grown-up" shopping in Lorca was that Kathy had wanted to buy some saucepans. When we had left the house in August we left behind everything we could think of to equip the house. Bearing in mind how hot August is we had lived on salads for two weeks – and hence neither of us had thought about the need of saucepans. Our younger son Paul and his girlfriend had gone down to the house in October with David and Edith, and, having settled in, they had set to prepare a chili con carne. They laid everything out and – at 6pm on a Saturday she went rifling through the cupboards looking for the saucepans. We received a phone call in England that evening to tell us that as they couldn't find our pans they had cooked the sauce in the grill pan from the oven, and cooked the rice in the microwave. It was then that Kathy realized we had none.

As the next day was Sunday and the shops were all shut for some *fiesta* or other on the Monday we arranged for them to borrow the necessary utensils from Keith and Vicki nearby. This trip to Lorca had been the appointed time to correct the situation and purchase our own pans. Having failed so conclusively, and having wasted so much energy and fuel I was determined to put things right, especially as I was fairly clear that I was the only one who had any doubt that it might all be my fault. We soon found ourselves back in Huercal Overa – the town whose market left us so unimpressed earlier that morning. This time though we approached from the other end of town and found ourselves at the tail end of a large and busy street market. I dropped Kathy off while I parked the car. Having parked I went in search of her and found that the first stall sold pans! So I did the obvious and negotiated hard to buy a set of brown enamel pans to regain my wife's affections. It seemed far more appropriate than flowers at the time. I then wandered deeper into the market and found Kathy looking thoroughly miserable and saying that as everything was closing up she didn't have time to choose. This was my chance to demonstrate my thoughtfulness, good negotiating skills and my affection – I presented her with the large white carrier bag containing the five pans of various sizes of which I was so proud. She burst into tears. It seemed that Kathy had other ideas about the sort of saucepans she wanted, and although she had not communicated these ideas to me I was obviously in the wrong for not knowing what she wanted. Moments later we were once again at the pan stall, only this time we were trying to negotiate a trade in of the goods purchased only a few minutes earlier. It took no time to establish that there was nothing there to meet Kathy's standards, and eventually she started to move into pragmatic mood and accept that these pans, selected so lovingly by her husband, are really rather rustic and fit quite well the country effect which we are trying to create.

Sundays and feast days do have another important purpose, apart that is from annoying the uninitiated. They are the time when all good folk assemble for fun and jollity. One such regular occurrence is the season of pig killing. Many families of the land keep a pig or two and traditionally they are slaughtered a few weeks before Christmas. Usually the first weekend in December is set aside for this ritual. It coincides with Constitution Day and for some areas the proximity to the festival of St Nicholas is also important. I never really did find out how St Nicholas, a Turkish bishop, came to be the old man in red cloak and white beard that we know as Santa Claus. Why would a bishop from warmer climes feel the need to dress in heavy winter robes? And how, under Dutch tradition, did he come to have a helper called Black Pete, who is apparently meant to be of Spanish origin?

Back though to the pig killing. The mother of the house usually tends the pig. This may be the owner's wife or even his mother in law. It is carefully fattened ready for the big day, which is planned with great care. Friends and family are invited, as are other key locals. Often the mayor himself will appear. As always at such an occasion large quantities of wine and other drinks are on offer – and most of it is consumed. The lady of the house also prepares a massive array of food, supplemented by every visitor, as each family will bring various dishes and bottles and baskets and tins. The tables creak – and by the end so do most of the participants. The party starts in daylight and finishes long after the sun has gone off to visit other parts of the world.

The poor animal in question is brought out of his pen to be admired by all, a frightening enough event I am sure. The children will pet it and feed it (rather pointless at this stage), and at an unseen signal those who are interested move with the pig and its owner to the side of the house. I understand that the discretion displayed in this description is not exhibited by every host, as some are dealt with in full gushing view. But once in place the animal is dispatched fairly rapidly with a sharp(ish) knife to the throat. Then comes the fun bit (excuse the irony) as everyone join in the job of butchery. Nothing is wasted, the head goes for brawn, the legs are hung to cure, the trotters and offal are all put to good use and the rest is jointed. Some people will only put pre-frozen food into their freezers, meaning that fresh meat continues to be treated just as it has always been. What cannot be cured or otherwise preserved must be eaten, and the amount of fresh meat coming from a full-grown pig demands that the joints are shared amongst the friends and neighbors. As a result it is quite normal to arrive with a green salad and depart with a handful of chops.

I remember one set of British friends saying that they would like to buy a pig for the freezer. They had often done so in England, but were afraid that over here it would arrive in one piece and probably on its own feet, creating very different emotions than all the neatly labeled freezer bags that their village butcher provided in Surrey.

The pig is killed on a Saturday and the celebrations and hangovers last until the Monday. For some Sunday is just a blur. One old boy reputedly woke up on a Tuesday morning with a headache that would crack your skull. He rolled over in bed and opened his eyes to find a pig's head staring back at him. As you might expect he swore never again to let alcohol pass his lips – well never on a Sunday at any rate.

26 - Out and About

Because the Spanish eat so late the wonderful creation of *tapas* serves a particular need for the northern European visitor. Not only do the locals eat dinner at a time when most true Englishmen are sipping their malted milk drinks and preparing for bed, they have a very different eating pattern throughout the day. Like so many of us these days they will leave home with no more than a cup of coffee - usually *café con leché* (coffee with frothy milk)- and they may well grab a pastry on the way to work. For some though their first solid food of the day will be a pastry or biscuit mid-morning. And traditionally a *copa* (glass) of red wine or even a *coñac* (Spanish brandy) might be taken to stir the spirits, probably accompanied by a cigarette.

At what we might consider to be lunchtime they are stuck into a day's work, and by the time they are ready for their midday meal it is actually mid-afternoon and those of us from colder climes are flagging. It is at times like these that *tapas* comes into its own. The Spanish will rarely drink for its own sake and normally eat when they drink. The concept of *tapas* covers a host of small dishes. Perhaps it helps to know the origin of the word and the idea. Firstly *tapas* comes from the Spanish verb for a cover (*una tapa*) and originates from the idea of covering a glass of wine with a small piece of bread to stop flying creatures and other impurities from contaminating an otherwise pure product. It was not uncommon for the drinker to finish off by eating the cover or *tapa* either for its own nourishment value or to get the combined effects of the bread and the wine soaked into it.

At Easter, while the building work was underway friends suggested we meet up for dinner in a nearby town after they had been to a local evening class. They chose a particular bar and there we, they and other friends had a glass before wandering off for dinner. By this time it was around 9pm, so really rather early by local standards to get too serious about an evening meal. They led us up one of the main streets and into an apparently residential area. Inside one of the official buildings we

saw a very different view to that seen by the students who sat examinations in the same room earlier the same day.
The desks were stacked in the entrance hall and in their place were tables and patio chairs. This was the ultimate example of working an asset, a government facility by day and a free enterprise undertaking by night. In the conversion they not only created an eating-house. They created a superb ethnic restaurant that would be packed every night if it were located on London's South Bank or in the Village in New York. It would also cost around $50 plus per head, and the wine list would start at $20 a bottle. Here we ate well, and we drank well. I was relieved that Kathy and I had only to stagger back to the hostal where we were staying at the time, because we sure as heck wouldn't have driven after that.
The son of the *patron* sang the menu to us. There was nothing to read and you had to be fairly cute to keep up with him. We bowed to friends' greater experience and better judgment and let them choose. The result was a constant stream of *tapas* dishes, which would have satisfied any appetite and even very discerning pallets. We ate fresh *gambas* (prawns), *callamares* (squid), *boquerones* (pickled anchovies), pork, fish, vegetables and some wonderful concoction of garlic, onion and potatoes. It just kept coming and every dish was even better than its predecessor.
At the end of the evening we had two shocks. The first was that the six of us had run up a bill amounting to under $6.50 a head, and this included all the food and the wine. The second that to get out we had to squeeze past or climb over the various tables which had been added since our arrival. As we were to discover later on the restaurant spills onto the paved area outside in summer to accommodate the crowds who wish to eat there. That on condition that you avoid the place during the almond harvest, because then, of course, it is closed to allow the staff to work in the fields. On a later visit we bumped into a Spanish friend who was shocked that any English incomers had found this pearl. He pointed out that this was a local secret and asked us to promise that we would not tell. So just which college and in which town I cannot say. But I can assure you that many other "secrets" lay hidden waiting to be found. If not by us then perhaps by you?
Today most bars, especially in the cities of other parts of the country and throughout Andalucía, offer at least a small selection of *tapas*. The choice may be no more than ham and cheese, or possibly salted almonds, but it is normal to find a selection of dishes of the sort that we enjoyed that night. They are usually displayed in a glass counter cabinet on white plates or in

terracotta dishes. The choice includes many nibbles. There are usually a few meat dishes, both cut meats and casseroled; and omelette, *tortilla,* is usually on the menu. It is not uncommon to find stuffed peppers or artichokes, fresh asparagus or tomatoes and onions finely sliced and sprinkled with oil.

The choice is as wide as the host's imagination and we uncover more ideas all the time. While *tapas* are a handy way to help down a drink or to bridge the gap between meals, the selection also provides the basis for a fun lunch. We often sit in a beach bar, or high in the hills enjoying the contrasts of view and the almost infinite variety of food on offer. It is quite possible to taste seven or eight different dishes in a light lunch, and for the passengers rather than the driver, to wash it all down with a glass or two of chilled beer or local wine. *Jamon y queso*, that quintessentially Spanish array of rough cut cured ham and tasty cheese, is all the better for a glass or two of *jérez*, and the sherry here tends to be of the tongue-tightening *fino* variety. The sweet or even medium sherry more familiar to the British taste is only now starting to appear in the areas where the British appear.

We explored the area quite widely on our various short visits while the house was being torn apart and re-built – there was little that we could do to help, other than get out of the way. On these outings we tested a wide selection of inexpensive eating places and found a host of "to be recommended" *tapas* bars. Our first find was the coast around the Murcian resort of Águilas. We drove through the Almanzora valley to join the coast north of Garrucha. The route passes through Cuevas del Almanzora, and we saw our first view of some of the cave dwellings, set up in the hills across the valley. We then traveled through rugged terrain along a road that was undergoing serious improvement. The road consisted of sections of magnificent new road blasted into the rocky hillsides interspersed with windy lanes and massive road works. Today of course the old windy sections have all been replaced or straightened out, and this route is a pleasant way down to the sea. We drove by the village of Los Lobos and in front of us glimpsed the sea. Just here there are a number of beautiful small coves and even in August we found them under-populated, even empty.

The first "resort" along here is S. Juan de los Terreros, which is in truth a collection of pleasant houses and a few villas along the coastal road, plus a few camp sites and a couple of supermarkets. There is a very pleasant *hostal* where we sometimes stop for a late morning coffee, and at the northern end there is the one hotel that legitimizes the description of S. Juan as a seaside resort. It is a super little seaside village, where families can be sure of a peaceful and relatively safe stay. S. Juan does not appear in most guidebooks and I am sure that none of its devotees will thank me for mentioning its existence. It is the most northern coastal resort in Almería, and indeed the most northern Mediterranean resort in Andalucía.

Just across the provincial border in Murcia sits the larger seaside town of Águilas. This is a very pleasant small town, which has been bypassed with a main road to Lorca, removing all but local traffic from a delightful vacation spot. Like many Spanish resorts Águilas is situated on a headland, with fortifications designed to keep a watching eye over potential invaders arriving by sea. As in the other resorts with a similar geography the town boasts two beaches, one either side of the headland. The best known vacation spot with such a location is Benidorm, where the long eastern beach to the left of the headland is known as the *Levante* (sunrise) beach, reflecting its eastern aspect, while the more recently developed sister on the western side is known as the *Poniente* (sunset). Those descriptive names are also used in the other resorts that share the same sort of split, including Calpé, the smaller brother to Benidorm, just a short drive north.

In Águilas though the visitor can still find a town, which must reflect what Benidorm would have looked like 40 years ago - or more. For most of its length the *Poniente* beach is bordered by a pedestrian *paseo* (sidewalk) with private houses, apartments and a few bars alongside. The beach still has palm trees growing in suitable places to provide much appreciated natural shade from the mid-day sun. And the bars set tables across the pavement allowing customers to sit at the edge of the beach with a drink in hand, under a parasol, while sampling the local *tapas*. In one of these bars some enterprising individual has patiently built three large three-dimensional jigsaws, including the Eiffel Tower. Even in the most local parts of the Spanish *costas* there is a cosmopolitan air to be found.

Águilas is not just pleasant; it also boasts some architectural gems, both constructed and industrial. The old fishing harbor has been extended to allow better road access and to provide a small private vessel marina. As the port is set in the shadow of the headland it is effectively in the centre of this little town. And right opposite, at the start of the *Levante* beach, is an old steam engine, marking the role of the railway in creating tourism on this stretch of the *costa*. In fact, as in so many other places, without the iron way there would be many gaps in the tourist maps. The railway from Granada towards the eastern coast and the line running south from Murcia met in Lorca, from where certain trains continued to the coastal terminus in Águilas. Lorca has a similar, possibly identical engine at the northern approach to the town. I know this because whenever we have chosen to explore Lorca (and found it shut) we have passed this example in one direction or another on our way into or out of the town.

The industrial architecture is interesting, but some of architectural features in the buildings of Águilas are exceptional. The old casino building is like many of those in smaller late 19th century Spanish resorts, and demonstrates the affluence once boasted by these towns and their visitors. But this town still has some other gems, which would have been destroyed had Águilas had dramatic growth in tourism inflicted upon it in the sixties and seventies. One example is the consistory offices in the old square, located just behind the headland. It has the most exquisite Moorish style carved façade I can remember. In dark red, weathered stone, highlighted by lighter sections it demonstrates enormous skill and pride – on the part of both architect and craftsmen. On another side of this same *plaza* are two impressive bank buildings. These are the sort of branch offices built to welcome and accommodate large deposits, demonstrating once again the wealth that once resided here.

Of the other structural attractions here one, which fascinates Kathy each time we visit, is the tropical birdcage in a park opposite to the casino. Here caged birds are on display in an enormous aviary. The unusual aspect of this particular cage though is that through careful and discreet nibbling the generations of small birds living there have created a private exit. So private that the keepers have obviously failed to find it. These little finches and the like fly in and out of the cage without restriction, and even seem to act as "runners" for the bigger birds who have failed to find a way out. Watching them we could not see how they did it, but we had to accept that birds taking food out of our hands on the outside of the cage appeared inside moments later, and shared their spoils with the other inhabitants. There was no attempt to prevent this charitable distribution of aid, and the visitors, especially the children, came from a fair distance just to see this slight of wing performed. David Copperfield, or perhaps the great Harry Houdini might have taught these creatures the tricks of escapology.

At the southern end of the eastern coast of Almería is the *Parque Natural de Cabo de Gata-Nijar*. Here wildfowl exist in a protected environment and provide immense pleasure to visitors. The

safeguarded nature of the cape is important as a home to local bird life, but also as a stopping off place for migratory birds travelling between summer territories in northern Europe and winter in the warmer climes of Africa. In summer visitors can see many hundreds of greater flamingos in temporary residence. Regrettably there are no recorded breeding pairs, but the sight in the area of Las Salinas, is well worth a visit. The saltpans are still exploited commercially and provide what seems to be a most attractive home for breeding birds.
This is an ornithologist's paradise and here a good pair of binoculars will repay their cost in the pleasure they bring. A host a species visits to breed, including osprey and storks. Others include herons and terns, and a collection of rarer gulls also visits this southeastern corner of the Iberian Peninsular. The birds are certainly the major feature of this park, but reptile lovers may also be rewarded, as there are various lizards and grass snakes and vipers to be found. The lizards include the Italian wall lizard, found no-where else in Spain. Foxes and hares live here in some degree of safety and Mediterranean monk seals are slowly re-establishing themselves in the Cabo de Gata after a period of over 20 years since last breeding here.
The park covers nearly 70,000 acres, and the topography is divided into two distinct styles. The Sierra de Cabo de Gata is made up of volcanic matter and it is still possible to see some laval columns, but the second aspect, the dunes, are at least as outstanding, partly because of the changing nature of the coastal strip. The dunes along the seafront are constantly changing as the waters and winds create erosion and deposit. Behind them sit salty lagoons, and further inland a more permanent group of dunes, kept in place by the plant life growing over them.
We decided to visit the park on a quieter day, not wanting to be over-run by coach parties. To get to the wildfowl areas we had to do what comes so easily to the Spanish, yet so hard to the British. We had to disobey authority. We were told to head for the lifeguards tower, which is situated alongside the coast road. Right opposite there is a sign, which reads "*Entrada Prohibida*" (no entry). Good, law-abiding English folk that we are it was clear that our quest was to be frustrated by officialdom. The sign is not new, so obviously it had been impossible for some time to cross this un-gated boundary. The Spanish think differently about these things. They know that the sign is official. They know that it means they should not enter. But they also know that as long as they do no harm no one will take any action against them.

We watched a Spanish family drove straight past as I was turning round to drive away - and I wondered what would happen. They weren't stopped and nothing unspeakable seemed to happen to either them or their car. So rather than drive away unfulfilled - I decided to wait a little while, just in case they got away with it. There were no sirens, and no sign of security forces raiding their little old Seat Panda. Then another car - a German BMW - drove straight through. Well if it was OK for the Germans it must be OK for us I decided. And so I probably broke the law - and got away with it. On the other side of the no entry sign is a car park. This was obviously constructed for the purpose of parking cars, and yet, to my simple English mind, cars were prohibited from entering. This is a complex conundrum, which requires a serious change of mindset to be accepted. Next to the car park is the purpose built hide, which overlooks the *Salinas*, and provides the most wonderful views of the birds. This is the most relaxing way to spend a few hours, and to those philistines who say that Spain is only Benidorm and Torremolinos I say, "Get out and about. Visit the *Cabo de Gata* and see if you still feel that way."

27 - Sights for sore eyes

The views across the mountains are amazing, but there are other interesting sights to be seen here as well. For years, as we have driven through Spain, I have been intrigued by the sight of older Italian registered cars heavily loaded heading down the A7, the coastal highway, which links southern Spain with France and beyond. Somehow the phrase "heavily loaded" does not do full justice to the ingenuity of the drivers of these vehicles. It is not unusual to see a very old Fiat 127 loaded with bundles and cases inside and with three-piece suite, a bed or a fridge strapped to the roof. In some cases the bits strapped to car are as large as the car itself, posing, you might think, a fair degree of risk. Yet no one seems to take any notice.

The traffic police are really only interested in speeding motorists or those actually involved in accidents. By the time an accident happens there is no chance of preventing it, and these cars certainly aren't about to break the 70 mile speed limit. So they don't get stopped. See them on an exposed stretch of motorway around Valencia in strong winds though and you will be sure to ask why. Under these conditions or in an emergency stop the driver looses a large degree of control. He is already driving a car designed to sit around 4 inches higher, and by now not only is the suspension almost completely compressed, but the bodywork only escapes contact with the tires if the driver continues in a straight line and brakes gently.

I have asked several Spanish friends what these vehicles represent and we have come up with countless explanations. We eventually settled on the obvious reason, these Italian tourists were vacationing on the cheap. They were renting unfurnished accommodation and were transporting the essentials with them. Indeed I had heard that in some less savory parts it was unwise to leave furniture in a house when one traveled for fear of burglary, so perhaps this exercise served the dual purpose of securing one's belongings, while providing a home away from home.

This year, as we have been travelling more frequently, we noticed a few further clues that would seem to scupper that idea. Firstly these over-loaded vehicles are often occupied by just the driver. This must be a very lonely sort of vacationer – unless the family had flown on ahead. Secondly I don't remember seeing the same burdened vehicles heading north at the end of their personally furnished breaks. Indeed I don't remember seeing many Italian registered cars heading north in any condition, occupied or not; loaded or not. So perhaps there was a new enclave of Italians setting up residence in Southern Spain. But there is no apparent evidence other than the mysterious disappearing cars loaded to bridge height.

It was a colleague from Milan who explained the phenomenon and in doing so satisfied the curiosity of Spanish colleagues and various friends, who had become as intrigued as us. It seems that there are still large numbers of "guest workers" of Moroccan origin living in the industrial northern cities of Italy. Milan and Turin have benefited from their hard labors for many years. The main objective of their work is to keep their families, many still living at home in Morocco, and to set aside the resources to permit eventual retirement back in their native lands. They tend to store up their leave entitlement and take a three or four-week breaks. This involves leaving work at the end of a busy day and then driving non-stop in seriously over-loaded and unsuitable cars, from the heart of Northern Italy, along the French Mediterranean coast and the length of Spain. They do this with minimum stops and very little sleep, because their target is to catch the overnight ferry the following evening from Almería or another port. Worse still some will drive on the Gibraltar or Cadiz to take the short sea crossing, guaranteeing no sleep in the whole journey, which might take 36 hours.

Presumably they drive in high expectation of the welcome awaiting their return, and it is just adrenaline which keeps them going. This seems to me to be a classic case of travelling in anticipation, and a particularly dangerous one at that. We have seen a few of these vehicles overturned at the roadside and I can only assume that those that survive the journey do so mainly by luck. The scene is rather like those tiny birds that fly halfway across Europe and then halfway down the length of Africa for a few months in the sun, only to return with summer to breed another brood to undertake the same hazardous journey the following year. From my perspective both are travelling against the odds, but love and loyalty are great motivators, and in both cases these factors seem to guarantee an added energy, which, for most at least, helps to ensure success.

The sights to be seen in this region are beautiful and awe inspiring, with a few of the usual nasties along the way. We do have fly tips around us, and the local elections in May were won

by a new Mayor who promised to clean up. Almost within days of winning new refuse bins appeared all along every road in and out of the town. Up until this point there were no more than half a dozen bins on the road from our house into town. Now it seemed we had to dodge them in a slalom style run. They were on every corner, and there was no excuse for dumping rubbish in the ravines or at the roadside. Don't get me wrong the streets were not festering with putrid remains. But there was a tendency amongst some to get rid of their old sinks and tumble dryers in the nearest convenient gully.
Now things were being sorted at last and smart green rubbish bins appeared everywhere. The manufacturers probably paid out bonuses on the basis of this contract alone. But some residents were less than happy. No one objected to the idea of cleaning up, but there were objections raised to the expense. Hard earned and much resented taxes were being squandered on over populous green plastic bins. Others objected to having litter containers being positioned outside their houses. What a reputation. As a result the bins moved, as if by magic, and when the refuse men called very few of the containers were where they were meant to be. For while they tried to repatriate them to their original locations. After a few vain attempts they gave up and learned to accept the spots chosen by the villagers – even where this meant three bins pushed together in one spot. The locals did have the common sense to position some of these new containers in the spots most commonly associated with the fly tipping. These bins, like their aluminum predecessors, are around 6 feet long, by a three feet deep and about four feet six high. They are of the type found outside small industrial units or larger restaurants, and are the means by which all domestic refuse is collected here.
There is no such thing as a weekly house-to-house collection, and hence no disputes about rubbish being spilled on the drive. There is no risk of getting the neighbors smelly bin in error, and the bin men cannot refuse to collect your extra bag on the occasions when you forget to put the bin out the week before. Most people, even in our rural community now live within a short stroll of a bin, and have no excuse for not using it. And collections are frequent. Kathy's parents' bins are emptied every evening, and the bins are disinfected frequently. While ours aren't cleared quite as often the twice-weekly collection is a contrast to some UK local authorities, which now restrict collections to once a fortnight. The result is a cleaner and

healthier environment, and I have to say that new Mayor seems to have read this one well.

Almería does not have as many of those picture-book hill top villages where the white painted houses sit in layers and reflect the sun to create a magnificent spectacle. As a result those that exist are all the more outstanding. Sorbas on the old road to Almería city is built above a ravine and the houses on the edge command the most wonderful views. This spot though was not chosen because of the enjoyable vista. It was selected because of the ease of defense. As invaders headed inland from the coast they could be seen far enough away to allow the locals to erect their final fortifications and place adequate guards to defend their homes. Today the mediaeval structures are occupied by banks and council offices, and one or two by bars and restaurants. But they have a special appeal to visitors who can wander the narrow streets. We made the mistake on our first visit of parking in a side street, which required us to exit through a maze of narrow roads, where each encounter with another car presented a fresh challenge and another set of disapproving looks. We could see them saying – "More foreigners!"

While Sorbas is an impressive oasis on the edge of the desert, the most famous Almerían hilltop village is Mojácar. There are two sides to Mojácar. The modern Mojácar Playa is a small but well equipped seaside resort. It was introduced to the UK package vacation market in the early 1970s by the now defunct Horizon Holidays. Although it has grown since then it still maintains the air of a rather select resort. The beach is the focus, and because the sands run for miles the development has been along its edge. Usually it reaches no more than a block inland, and there are still bamboo shaded beach bars serving *tapas* and drinks to the families who frequent the beach.

To the northern end the resort almost reaches the slightly classier Garrucha, with a small underdeveloped marina and some fine seafood restaurants. Between Garrucha and Mojacar is a cluster of golf course and tennis club, appealing to the international set.

Mojacar has a few fine eateries, and Kathy's parents, David and Edith were pleased to be able to take us to a restaurant, which they had found on an earlier visit with their friends. The *Virgen del Mar* is part of a hotel of the same name. It sits across the quiet coastal road and leads onto the beach. David was especially impressed by the mussels, which we enjoyed to the accompaniment of a band of strolling players – students we guess - who played fine flamenco, dressed in medieval style costumes, enhanced by Raybans and Nike shoes.

But it is Old Mojácar that provides the white hill village view so typical of other parts of Andalucía. It is typically Moorish in design. The houses are like small white blocks, everyone clean and recently whitewashed. There are Arab style gateways into the town, and the layout is reminiscent of a North African souk, except for the absence of pungent smells, and the almost hassle free shopkeepers. Here the *indalo* symbol is common. This stick man holding a halo type semi-circle above his head is probably Neolithic in origin. The best guess is that they first appeared in the cave dwellings further north in the province, but to this day they are displayed outside houses to ward off bad luck.

Mojácar has history that dates back to pre-Roman times, when it was an important trading point and was known as *Murgis*. It was the Moors who changed the name to something akin to the present day Mojácar. They defended their settlement against the kings who were Catholic by faith and only accepted rule by Christian monarchs once they gained authority to practice their own faith and customs. Before the Civil War Mojácar had a population of nearly 10,000, which dropped to just a few hundred in the 1950s. Before Horizon arrived with their package vacationers this little spot had been found by an intellectual set. It was the award to Mojácar of the title "Spain's Prettiest Village" which brought the village to the attention of Vladimir Raitz who founded Horizon, and the arrival of vacationers, which persuaded the writers and artists to seek inspiration elsewhere.

As a result there are genuine artists houses available for vacation rentals, and many of them have breathtaking views. They require a fairly strong constitution; because being built on a hillside these quaint houses are all accessed by means of steep winding streets. Vehicles can only reach certain parts of the village, and mostly must be parked on the edge, leaving driver and passengers to climb the final part of the journey. This can be rather a testing climb, especially if you've just done the monthly shop at the food store. Mojácar also has one of the weekly markets for which Spain is so famous, and this one operates in the windy streets of the hill village. The stalls are propped up at one end to make the counters level, and stallholders stand all day with one leg bent at the knee to stop them leaning over – this in itself is quite a strain. But just watching the tourists puffing their way around can be quite a tiring exercise. It is especially wearing when you see the little old ladies in black from head to toe nipping around as if there weren't a hill in sight.

Back in the north of the province the sanctuary at the *Saliente* provides a magnificent view, and now some enterprising local entrepreneurs have recognized the commercial value in that view. Just below the mediaeval structure they are erecting a new hotel, which will have terraces looking straight down the gorge. I wonder if they will resist the temptation to name the property *Vista Allegré*. When Kathy and I first visited Mijas on the Costa del Sol the bit that really impressed me was the view from the terrace of the Hotel Mijas. It was on the road up from the coast and high enough to look over the construction out to sea. This new development in the *Sierra de las Estancias* will have equally outstanding views. The clientele will have to be different because day-trippers from the coast in search of a quiet beer are hardly likely to venture this far, but it will provide a wonderful retreat for anyone looking for a few days away from it all.
These hills have been an important part of our lives. When our son Paul and his girlfriend visited the house with David and Edith they ventured off into the hills in search of solitude and each other. Mark on his visit to us in August decided to wake his system up with a run. He disappeared over the hill immediately behind us and down into the ravine. From there he climbed nearly a hundred yards at running pace and returned to us about half an hour later hot and exhausted. He had certainly got his system going again, and dropped into a chair with a large glass of fresh spring water – he was a real sight for sore eyes!

28 - House Warming

Just over a year after our decision to buy Cortijo La Higuera we arrived for a one-week stay. For the first time we were able to walk straight in to find our furniture as we had left it and the cupboards stocked. But when we had left in August the house was protecting us from the heat outside, and by night we slept with the windows open to encourage some cooler air inside. This time we arrived from the airport and drove up to the house at around 10pm on a cold and very dark November Saturday. We had left behind a dismal storm in England and were looking forward to some sunshine. What we saw was the aftermath of strong winds and snowstorms. The moon was almost full that night and the sky was clear, and as a result we had a good view of snow on the peaks as we drove higher from the *autovia*.

By the time we reached Las Pocicas it was obvious that we were not to be welcomed by a warm house. Still that wouldn't be a problem. We had gas bottles to heat the water and run the stove. We had a couple of sacks of logs to burn on the fire and we had a small fan heater. This we had bought the previous winter while we were staying at Apollonia's hostel. Because her property is built high on the side of the central ravine in Albox it is exposed to the winds and especially to the chilling winter winds. So we arrived tired and cold and were pleased with what we found. The key still worked in the door and inside everything was just as we had left it. Paul's visit had not left a mark and the builders had completed most of the outstanding jobs. They had created quite a bit of dust in the process, but then that is only to be expected. Unfortunately we had not thought to put some protection behind the beautiful lattice crafted cupboard doors, with the result that the dust and sawdust had accumulated in these cupboards, on, between and even in the crockery, cutlery and provisions which we stored there.

The one thing that we were not prepared for was the cold. It should have been no surprise really. The walls are immensely thick, purposely so to provide insulation against both summer sun and winter chill. However they are so thick that the daytime sun of winter cannot penetrate the house. The breeze outside was bitter, and I decide that the first job was to re-connect the liquid petroleum gas canister. We have a small *cabana* (cabin) outside the kitchen door where these gas bottles are stored. I tried four times to connect the regulator and my hands were freezing. Kathy tried and got no further.

We decided to do the obvious and telephone her parents. This would give us the chance to tell them that we had arrived and to seek advice on the gas bottles. While Kathy went to phone I plugged in the electric fan heater. Neither was working. Well that's not quite true. The electric fire made all the right noises and expelled varying quantities of tepid air. Regrettably it was not powerful enough to cut through the bitter temperature as the walls were radiating ice cold. The phone on the other hand just wasn't working. No signal - Nothing. Fortunately we also have a local mobile telephone, unfortunately though it only works in a few "hot spots" in the house. The best reception is out on the new terrace, and so Kathy stood in the dark amid bitter winds, her teeth chattering, and taking instructions from her father.

I did as I was instructed. The sign that the regulator and the bottle have connected is that you can lift the bottle off the ground by holding the regulator. Every time I lifted the regulator the bottle stayed behind. I just wasn't getting the knack of this. By now it was approaching 11pm and we were getting colder rather than warmer. I decided that lighting the open fire would do little good as the sitting room door is around 40 feet away from the bedroom door, and if we were ever to heat the sitting room we would not stand a single chance of heating any other room. The one major job that was still outstanding at this point was the wood-burning stove, which should have been fitted in the dining room. Had this been in place we could have had an almost immediate effect on the temperature. But it was not.

We had bought one blanket for our bed before departing in August – forward thinking. So we lay this over the icy bed, wrapped up in layers of clothes so that we could remove them as we warmed up over night and left the useless fan heater running as we went to bed. I did no more than clean my teeth, on the basis that I would fix the gas and enjoy a warm shower next morning. As you might expect we did not sleep well. We cuddled, we shivered, we consoled each other, but we did not sleep.

We were up quite early. There wasn't much point in staying in the cold. Thank goodness it was not also damp. I went straight to the gas bottles and continued to fail for a further 20 minutes.

Then, in temper, I struck the black collar around the regulator and there was a sort of click. I lifted the now very heavy regulator and the bottle came with it. "Oh yes Dad said something about pushing the collar down," said Kathy. "Thank you," said I.
We now had a stove and hot water. It felt as if we had survived several months of bitter cold. The fact that we had arrived in a heated car only 10 hours earlier didn't seem possible somehow. It was now warmer outside than in, as the sun started to heat up the air, and we decided to go off in search of more heating and a further supply of logs. The firewood that we had so far had been picked up for us by David, and "imported" from Torrevieja. As we were going out there was no sense in leaving a burning fire behind us - apart from anything it would hardly be safe. So we left our ice block and headed into town - on a winter's Sunday.
Everything was closed - of course. And I do mean everything. We couldn't even find a bar to buy a cup of coffee. So we drove on. I stopped at a local petrol station and was amused to see that they had good stocks of pre-packed ice, but no firewood. We continued in the direction of the coast. Surely we would find a few shops open in Vera or Mojacar. We found one - a general store of the sort you find on campsites, and were confident that here we would find fuel. We were wrong. At this point we remembered that we had invited twenty or so people to join us for our housewarming on the Tuesday, and realized that, based on previous experience, and taking the housewarming into account, Monday would almost certainly be a public holiday.
On the way back we found another fuel station that did sell firewood. They had just two sacks, and so we bought them both. We now had one open fire, four bags of logs and a very large cold house to heat. We decided that our next stop should be to eat and so, having wasted yet more hours we stopped off at a new restaurant near to the Arboleas junction and enjoyed a hot meal in a warm dining room. It cost the usual exorbitant 1000 pesetas each - around $6.50 for a three course eal and wine. We then headed back and lit the fire. It did a good job of heating the sitting room, but as soon as we opened the doors to let the heat into other parts of the house we lost the benefit in our living room.
We lit the stove and let that raise the temperature in the kitchen, but it was increasingly clear that we must heat the whole house to raise the temperature of the walls; once we could achieve that we were sure that we could benefit from radiated heat. We were right, but it took some time to achieve. That day we sat in the

sun, while a fire blazed away inside to raise the ambient temperature. That evening we settled for warm soup and set off to our chilly bed early with a hot *lumumba* each to warm our way. *Lumumba* is a cocktail of uncertain origin, but traditionally made of hot chocolate liberally laced with white rum or brandy. The name sounds Caribbean, but the concoction is probably the invention of some barman in a modern resort hotel. That night it helped and as we were warmer when we climbed into our icy bed we made a better job of warming it.

The next morning we set off certain that everywhere would be closed yet again. After all it was Monday and more importantly we had shopping that we wanted to do. We were to be pleasantly surprised. The first stop was the bank, which was open, boding well for the rest. Having established that our funds had transferred intact I made a modest withdrawal and we headed over the bridge to the local Repsol depot. All the liquefied petroleum gas (LPG) sold in Spain is under the control of Repsol or Cepsa, with prices controlled by the government. Prices reflect very accurately the movements in market. When crude prices go up, so do LPG prices in Spain. But, and this bit is amazing to those of living elsewhere, when crude oil prices go down, so do the prices of gas.

We did the unthinkable and just said that we wanted two bottled gas fires, fitted and ready to work. We wanted them now and we didn't even try to haggle over the price. At this point I forgot all about asking for the *precio de offerta.* A few days later I had the chance to find out just how much I had been rooked by when we visited Hiper Olé. There I found a selection of similar fires. They offered four models, all looked quite nice and the one that we had bought was almost identical to the most expensive on offer. I could have saved the 4,000 pesetas difference on each one had I chosen the cheapest model here. Well not so actually because our fire may have been all but identical to the most expensive model, but it cost no more than the cheapest. It also had the advantage that it was real plug and play technology. Now that I knew how to push the collar into place I had them both burning in no time. Had we purchased at the supermarket we would then have had to go to Repsol to purchase the necessary gas bottles. The Repsol office staff would have checked the fires to ensure that they were safe and new contracts would have been needed. As it was we did the whole transaction in one easy move, our acquisitions worked almost instantly and we got a bargain. It almost always pays to shop around, but this time, almost by accident, we got it right first time.

Under Latin Skies

That same day, following one phone call, our wood burning stove was installed, and although we could not yet light it we were getting closer to being warm. On Monday evening we lit our two gas fires and the open fire and the temperature started to climb. I phoned David and asked him to stick a couple of sacks of logs in the boot of his car to bring with them to our housewarming next day. We were on a roll now, and by the end of the week our house would be warm. The best bit of advice we had though was from Keith who advised us to buy a couple of hot water bottles in the 100 *peseta* shop near to the *Notario* office. So on Tuesday morning I picked up bread fresh from our village bakers and the final provisions from Albox market. I also popped into the relevant 100 *peseta* shop and acquired a further and very thick blanket on the market.

It was difficult to reconcile just how cold the house was inside with the glorious warmth of the sun. I sat for a while over a cup of coffee at a pavement table outside one of the many bars in town, and I was so hot that I had to take off my jumper. Yet at the same time Kathy was at home teeth chattering. Or so I thought. By the time I returned she had the open fire raging and both gas fires burning at full power, and she had wisely turned the oven to its highest temperature to pump out more heat. The house was starting to come alive. I had also managed to lay my hands on an oil filled electric radiator and now we could risk a visit to the bathroom without fear of frostbite. This latest purchase also meant that we could dry ourselves with warm towels – this was luxury.

And to our great surprise the *Teléfonica* engineer had arrived. Our phone was originally installed in less than 30 minutes. By the miracles of modern science we were connected not by wires but by radio. In fact the telephone in our house uses the same technology as old analogue mobile phones. This means that with a power supply and a decent position telephones can be installed anywhere. I don't know how the Spanish do it. We still can't get decent reception in Hampshire, where the population is many times denser than here in the mountains. In fact to get reception on most mobile phones you have to walk or drive out of the village. This is a great, and entirely honest, excuse for being out of touch. But it can be a great inconvenience.

I watched the engineer as he tested all the bits of the equipment. We have two boxes on the wall, each about the size of a cream cracker packet, one sitting on top of the other. On top of the upper box is a small antenna. He checked each box and the back up power supply and he tried various alternative antennae. In the end he replaced a circuit board and the phone has been working just fine ever since.

As the week progressed and we were able to light the new wood burning stove the house started to absorb the heat generated and to radiate it back to us. It was becoming increasingly difficult to leave our farmhouse at the end of each stay, and this time it was extra hard because we knew that the heat, which we had put into the house, would gradually drain away over the following days. What started the week as an icebox was, by the end, a cozy warm home. We visited friends that week and added a few more personal touches to our home. But on several evenings we just enjoyed snuggling up around the fire and then after a nightcap climbing into our pre-warmed bed.

The electricity bill did climb a little that week, but the critical achievement was finding a suitable supply of firewood. The petrol station in Vera is a useful emergency stockist, but a decent supply at their prices would have been unrealistic. Most of our neighbors just burn the old trees and prunings from their own land, but of course we had handed over our responsibilities to others. As a result the wood was theirs not ours. We did though discover that the trailers full of logs parked alongside the weekly market were for sale. We certainly did not want the tons of logs that a load would comprise and so we asked around. We were lucky - again. With the help of our builder a very large supply was delivered in time for our next visit.

As a result the house is easily heated these days and it is a simple matter to maintain the warmth. I still ought to find a suitable place to store all these logs though. There's no point in tempting any light fingered home owner who might arrive late on a chilly Saturday night in search of something for a housewarming.

29 - Nothing to worry about

On a warm spring day we set off in search of local touches for our new home and headed for the pretty little village of Nijar. It sits near to the *autovia*, roughly half way to Almería. One day it may well be overshadowed by the needs of the modern traveler, as the neighboring highway junction has been earmarked as the access point to the planned new airport for Almería. The present airport is on the edge of the urban sprawl of Almería city, and it is blocking the developers' ambitions. This one is like many leisure airports in that it developed on the site of a military airfield. To this day the air force occupies one end of the field, while the civil air terminal sits at the other.

Nijar is known for the pottery and weaving created and sold here, and the main street of this little community is lined on either side with shops stocked high with pots, rugs, jumpers and so on. There is clearly a commercial streak in the way this place operates, but these little businesses are certainly not exploitative and every item on offer represents real value for money. These goods are also attractive in that they are so unusual. While the normal garden pots and troughs are on offer, so too are some designs not available elsewhere. The experts on The Antiques Road Show often describe various pottery and porcelain by the place of origin, or the factory name, "Delftware" or "Denbyware" for example. I feel sure that they would not have heard of "Nijarware", yet they are the poorer for this lack of knowledge.

On our first visit to Nijar we bought a couple of ethnic jumpers for the boys, but our "best buy" was a rug on *offerta.* I'm not sure how large a rug has to before it technically becomes a carpet, but this one was probably on the border. At around 10 feet by 8 feet it makes an impressive carpet in front of the sitting room fireplace. It has a large checkered pattern, just nine blocks of tints. The colors are all soft shades of nature and this rug (or should that be carpet) sets the room off perfectly. We had a really good day the time we first visited Nijar. Everything went wonderfully well and we coasted home without a care in the world. Gordon was right – there really was nothing to worry about.

When our guests started to arrive on that November Tuesday for our official housewarming, that carpet was the subject of many complements. The locals of course knew the style well. They told us how wise we were to choose *un alfombra de Nijar.* I am sure that they would have been polite if our floor covering had come from elsewhere, but it seemed that a carpet from Nijar showed real taste.

We had a really enjoyable afternoon. The sun shone gloriously and, although the house was by this time warming nicely, we all sat out on the terrace to soak up the warmth. Andréas and his wife Maria arrived with two gallon flagons of his homemade wine. This had the added flavor of aniseed, acquired from the previous contents of the glass containers, which still bore the labels for *anis*. I took them from him with gratitude – and then made the awful mistake of not serving it. He is a good friend and took it well, but to ignore a gift in that way is unkind. David and Edith arrived from Torrevieja with "rent a mob". We had invited a few of our friends to join us as they had given us inspiration and encouragement in our venture at times when we needed it most. And of course we invited Howard and Carmel, as without his article in the newspaper we would never have thought of looking in this corner of heaven.

Unexpectedly they brought gifts with them, including food for the party and various consumables, plus a terracotta wine rack, which I set up with pride in the scullery. It holds a dozen bottles, and I make it my personal quest to use the contents in strict rotation – when one bottle is emptied we open another. Well we wouldn't want to offend now would we? The other present – the highlight of the afternoon was given to us by our friends Vicki and Keith. They walked up the drive with Andréas and Maria and John, who lives across the road. They carried Andréas' flagons of wine and a fig tree. They had researched the subject carefully and established that *Rey de Higueras*, or King of Figs, was the tree to have. It produced the finest green fruit, the type which the Spanish and Italians serve with finely cut cured ham.

They had hunted for this tree and found it on Albox market. Keith then consulted Andréas to find the best spot to plant it, and under his advice we settled on a space in the middle of one of our lower fields. Keith was dispatched home to collect suitable implements for the planting, as I had none. When he returned Andréas was unhappy with the choice of tools and strode off down to his own tool shed to collect a mattock. For a man who has recently undergone major open-heart surgery he still puts a lot of energy into the things he does, and he first marked the size of the hole that had to be dug and then showed us how to break up the earth with the mattock before shoveling away the resulting soil. Several of us joined in the exercise, and before long we had dug a hole which we were satisfied would meet the requirements. *"Mas,"* instructed Andréas, who was supervising our work. More we dug and still more. At this point our mentor told us that it was not really as large as he would wish, but that he could accept it if we were too weak to dig any further. We settled for that endorsement of the hole that we had dug, which by now was around 6 feet in diameter and three feet deep. The tree was placed in its new home only after the bottom of the hole had been suitably broken up to provide soft enough soil for the roots to grow.

Then came the job of watering. And this presented us with a new problem. My hose was around 30 feet too short to reach the tree. We started to fill our only bucket and pass it down the hill, but this was not fast enough and provided far from the requisite quantity of water. So next I stood precariously on the hill holding the hose high to allow the spray to reach the tree. It did occasionally, but the winds decided to join the game and only around 25% of the water aimed at the moat dug around the tree actually made it. I was awaiting knee surgery at this time, an arthroscopy to remove the damaged cartilage – damaged while doing something just about as foolhardy as hanging of a steep hill while tugging at a hosepipe.

My knee was sore, well actually I was in agony, and gave way all too willingly when Keith offered to take over my hillside spot after I stumbled down. With the help of all these good friends our new tree was planted with great ceremony, and left in a pool of water to wallow overnight. I had strict instructions from Andréas to purchase an extension hose and a spade, and to water the tree again the next day. On the following day I was to fill in the moat and top water our new addition. Andréas also told me that now he would approve of us calling the house *La Higuera* as now we had a fig tree to match the name.

That evening we joined David & Edith and their friends for dinner. They were all staying at a nearby hostal, and as we were close to Edith's birthday we celebrated a successful housewarming and a birthday in style. The meal was taken from the 1000 *peseta* menu, served with house wine. We had a relaxed and pleasant evening, and fortunately we had been put in touch with a private hire driver who ran us there and back, so neither tiredness nor alcohol were a problem. We chatted over the day and were cheered by all the complements for our new home. We smiled at the tree planting ceremony, and with that inspiration ringing in my ears I decided to sort out the house sign.

Having made such a mess the first time I decided to do the job properly. I would strip off my first attempt and smooth off the wall before fixing new tiles with the correct adhesive. And I did! Next day I used a stone chisel to cut away the stones and uneven cement to give me a smoother surface. I then built up two layers of *cemento cola*, a fast drying grey cement mix, and left my new surface to set. I had carefully measured the space required and built a smooth background of just the right size for the new set of tiles. I had laid out the letters of *La Higuera* and carefully checked the measurements twice. The next day I re-measured the cement panel, which I had created and sure enough it was the correct size. So I nailed up a batten and proceeded to cement the tiles in place.

It worked. I was amazed, but it worked. The tiles went on smoothly. They now stand in a straight line and the cement panel behind was exactly the right size. I couldn't believe it. I don't do these things well. I have had a lifetime of messing up on DIY jobs – here I was looking at the name of our house in tiles placed by me. And I would be happy for anyone to run a hand over them – because I knew that they would comment on how well they had been fixed – not a nib in sight! Perhaps I can cope after all. So things were going well. The house was warm, the party had been a great success, Andréas approved of our new tree and had accepted the house name, and I had managed to fix the tiles for the house sign all on my own – and properly. There really was nothing to worry about.

That evening Kathy and I shared one of the better bottles of wine from amongst our housewarming presents and settled down in front of the fire with a couple of good books. We had not a care in the world – until about 3 o'clock in the morning that is. I woke up in a cold sweat amid the realization of what had happened. Our neighbors and our friends had provided us with a correctly planted, first class specimen of a fig tree. It was carefully chosen, as was its new home, and a team of us had worked hard to prepare the earth and to ensure that it was properly watered. And now it was my responsibility to look after this young tree. If anything were to go wrong now no one could doubt that it was my fault. Oh the responsibility – I couldn't get back to sleep that night for worry.

Who said there was nothing to worry about?

2030457

Made in the USA